A Defiant Celebration: Theological Ethics & Gay Sexuality

by

J. Michael Clark, M.Div., Ph.D.

Garland
Tangelwüld Press
1990

© 1990, J. Michael Clark

Library of Congress Cataloging-in-Publication Data

Clark, J. Michael (John Michael), 1953-
    A defiant celebration : theological ethics & gay sexuality / J.
Michael Clark.
        p.   cm.
    Includes bibliographical references.
    ISBN 0-934667-08-X ; $10.00
    1. Homosexuality--Religious aspects. 2. Gays--Religious life.
3. Sexual ethics. 4. Religious ethics.   I. Title.
BL65.H64C62   1990
241'.66--dc20   90-30837
                                                      CIP

For
Bob McNeir,
brother, lover, and friend,
and for
my whole extended family
of friends and lovers
who have taught me just how much
I still need to learn.

*   *   *

Acknowledgements

The author extends his appreciation to
**Mike Feinstein, Michael Greer, Bob McNeir,
Frank Puckett**, and **Steven Scanlon,**
for reading various earlier versions
of the present text;
many of their helpful comments and suggestions
have been incorporated herein.
Many thanks, --jmc

* * *

Table of Contents

✻ ✻ ✻

A
DEFIANT
CELEBRATION

J. Michael Clark

I. A Pilgrimage toward Celebration

Together, we set sail upon the stars,
into a realm where only the two of us exist,
a place carved out of night and away from day.

In the warmth of love's light,
hidden in cosmic darkness
far from all that binds us earthly,
we explore the numinous,
transcending roles in an alchemy
of tenderness and strength.

When the journey is done,
a two-in-oneness, we drift back,
laid in sleep on the arms
of a divine, cosmic embrace.

(for Steven, 1989)

In the wake of AIDS and AIDS hysteria during the 1980s, a small number of gay and lesbian religious writers began to exchange the defensive and apologetic style of previous work in religious studies for an assertive approach to the development of gay liberation theology (Boyd, 1987, Clark, 1987, 1989, Fortunato, 1987, Heyward, 1984, McNeill, 1988, Uhrig, 1984). As part of this movement, Malcolm Boyd founded an Institute for Gay Spirituality and Theology in California in 1987, and by 1988, both lesbians and gay men within the American Academy of Religion had formed officially recognized groups to pursue unapologetic gay/lesbian studies and dialogue in theology and religion. A further movement to undertake a specifically in-depth theological and/or ethical analysis of gay/lesbian sexuality, or of the myths and misunderstandings surrounding it, however, has been slower to emerge.

My own recent work (Clark, 1989), for example, examines both the writers cited above, as well as others, to join them theologically in reclaiming, reaffirming,

and celebrating gay/lesbian being. Yet, even the clear
affirmation and celebration of that text remains gener-
alized in its assertions about our sexuality. While
all gay/lesbian theologians implicitly or explicitly
assert that the issue for us is no longer that we are
gay, but how we are gay, neither my sources nor my own
work to date have explored the "how" in much detail,
apart from "safe sex" admonitions. A detailed synthesis of unabashed gay/lesbian sexual affirmation, in the
very face of AIDS and AIDS-redoubled homophobia, with
theological/ethical reflection has remained elusive.[1]
Now, as the gay and lesbian community(ies) move into
our third decade of gay/lesbian liberation and a second
decade of living with AIDS in the 1990s, such a defiant
celebration is long overdue.

Nelson (1978) reminds us that to pursue such a
celebration, to undertake theological and ethical reflection upon sexuality, is "genuinely exploratory";
citing Andre Maurois in his introduction, he comments,
"The need to express oneself in writing [on these
issues] springs from an unresolved inner conflict . . .
out of having discovered [a] problem and wanting a so-
lution" (p. 9). Drawing upon one's own subjective
wrestling with ethical issues in order to transform
private theological dilemmas into public theological
dialogue is an extension of the return to the phe-
nomenology of human experience--as a resource for theo-
logy--which Fackenheim (1968), Rubenstein (1966), and
various liberation and feminist theologians have been
advocating for more than two decades (cf., Clark,
1989). Rubenstein (1966) even goes so far as to say
that what the theologian is really doing is not pursuing some objective activity, but is rather "communicating an inner world he [sic.] suspects others may share"
(p. 246).

If the "vision of the theologian" can indeed be
legitimately affected and shaped by "the particularities of his or her experience" (Christ and Plaskow,
1979, p. 20), then gay liberation theology and any ethical reflections which stem from it will also require
phenomenological and even confessional resources
(Clark, 1989). Gay theology and ethics will be focused
upon the here and now particularities of gay people,
not only in the subjective experience of gay people
both communally and individually, but also in the subjectivity of each gay or lesbian theologian's own perceptions of, interpretations of, and participation in
gay life (Heyward, 1982, Clark, 1989). As both the
"communication of an inner world" and the "exegesis of

exegesis done . . . the doing of the exegesis of this time, the interpretation of our world and its days" (Neusner, 1979, p. 85), gay theology and ethical reflection will indeed depend heavily upon the individual theologian: It will derive from what I am struggling with and from what I come to believe, based upon and informed by my sources and my experience and interpretation of gay life, for which I alone, and not my sources, am ultimately responsible (Clark, 1989, cf., Heyward, 1984).

Gay theological and ethical reflection, as an activity, thus becomes a dialogue about personal understandings in order for us to discover commonalities and to celebrate differences in our thinking and experiencing. As such, our efforts are dynamic and provisional, and never authoritatively complete (Clark, 1989). Our reflective activity exists, instead, in the "morally ongoing openness" of mutuality, reciprocity, and dialogue (Heyward, 1984, p. 225). Or, as Heyward (1984) further explains, "Good constructive theology is done in the praxis of concrete situations, in which the doers of theology speak for and about themselves, rather than for and about others or humanity in general" (pp. 223-224, cf., Rubenstein, 1966). The modest particularity and the provisional sharing of gay theological and ethical reflection, as a dialogical activity, should also help us to avoid projecting any of that work upon another as "universally" true (cf., Heyward, 1984, Clark, 1989). In fact, the demand of particularity, coupled with the great diversity among gay/lesbian people, means we must avoid either universalizing our experience, or so particularizing our experience, in ways which exclude anyone. We must realize the partial, fragmented, and incomplete quality of what we do, acknowledging our diversity of gender, race, economic class, and life style, while continuing to struggle with concepts and issues which remain unclear or troublesome for us (Collins, 1981, Christ, 1979).

While we are thus compelled to agree with Collins (1979) that "nothing that is of us can be alien to our theology" (p. 152, emphasis added), including our sexuality in all its diversity of expression, we are also reminded by Ruether (1983a) that our subjectivity-as-resource must not emerge without a context, without both grounding and qualification. We cannot rely on mere subjectivity alone; we also require grounding in an "historical community and tradition" (p. 18). For us as gay/lesbian people, that demand itself is problematic. While Heyward (1984) argues that the effectiveness of theological and ethical reflection "rests on the extent to which we understand and trust our experience and our visions," she goes on to say that "we can do neither as long as we internalize the perceptions of reality that have been shaped historically for us by those whose interests fly in our faces" (p. 158). Specifically addressing the activity of developing gay/lesbian sexual ethics, Treblicot (1984) has similarly insisted that,

> . . . taking responsibility for [our] sexuality [doing sexual ethics] is not in the interest of patriarchy, which insists, for its own protection, that sexuality is only a given, that we have no role in creating it. [Patriarchal power] is maintained . . . not [by taking] responsibility for our own sexuality but, rather, [by attempting to act] on rules that are given to us. (p. 423)

More recently, McNeill (1988) has realized the extent to which a heterosexist, rule-constructed ethics works to sustain homophobia and gay/lesbian oppression. He writes that gay men and lesbians "are gradually becoming aware of the paranoid manipulations, fear, and hostility that surround them [and] they have begun to confront the evil structures that victimize them disguised as morality and the will of God" (p. 202). As gay/lesbian people undertaking the activity of theological and ethical reflection upon our sexuality, we are thus brought back to our collective historical experience of rootedness at the margins of our western Judaeo-Christian "historical community and tradition." As a result, we also come to realize that our very exclusion itself becomes a criticism of both scripture and tradition (cf., Christ, 1979, Ruether, 1985); that personal experience and traditional theological sources and norms always exist in tension for us (cf., Umansky, 1984); and thus, that gay liberation theology and ethics remain at odds with sexual and ethical givens, with the "a priori presuppositions of tradition" (Collins, 1981, p. 343). In short, our gay/lesbian theological and ethical reflections, particularly regarding our marginalized sexuality, must stand in a compassionately confrontational relationship with our western religio-moral heritage as we now claim our own authority for developing sexual ethics and for assuming responsibility for our sexuality. McNeill (1988) pointedly elaborates:

> Because of all the injustice with which we
> still have to contend, our efforts to achieve gay
> liberation must include a struggle against oppres-
> sive authority. . . . Liberation from oppression
> . . . that freedom, is something to be claimed,
> not something that is granted by external author-
> ity. (p. 204, emphasis added)

If, then, we are still going to attempt to engage
in theological and ethical reflection upon our sexuality, in a manner continuous with the Judaeo-Christian
tradition, we are consequently compelled to sift out
the liberating themes of steadfast love, of justice, of
love for neighbor, of a God who favors the outcast
(Ruether, 1983a), from the heterosexist and patriarchal
ideology of a religious heritage which has more often
sanctioned homophobia and gay genocide (Clark, 1989).
Given the critical/prophetic perspective of our historical exclusion from the institutionalized religious
"historical community and tradition," that very collective experience and perspective suggest that while the
tradition as mediated by scripture, doctrine, and dogma
may inform our theological and ethical work as resource, it no longer holds any oppressively binding
authority over us (cf., Clark, 1989). Given the particularly tenuous, or marginalized and critical, relationship of specifically gay theological and ethical
reflection to orthodox religious norms, such efforts
must remain at once continuous with, and yet at some
distance from, primary and often homophobic sources,
such as scripture or church documents. Gay theology
and ethics must continue responding to, reinterpreting,
and building upon/from secondary sources, those writers
who have already begun to recast primary sources into
liberational forms. Gay theology and ethics will thus
become another, tertiary layer--a further extension of
theological activity in the service of all people who
seek liberation and full humanity (Clark, 1989).
    In our theological and ethical reflection as
gay/lesbian people, then, we are called to synthesize
both our gay being and our gay sexuality with an often
homophobic and yet equally justice-seeking tradition,
and, in the process of effecting that synthesis, to derive our critical principles for doing theology and
ethics. Among those criteria will be an insistence
upon the right of gay/lesbian people to full humanity--
spiritually, sexually, sociopolitically, and medically.
Our theology will seek to nurture full humanity or
wholeness for gay people and ultimately for all people

(Clark, 1989, cf., Boyd, 1987). As such, gay theology and ethical reflection extend the work of liberation theologies historically to shift the focus from the vertical to the horizontal, to the here and now particularities of gay men and lesbians and of God's unabashed advocacy on our behalf, while simultaneously exhorting us to assume responsibility for active participation in our community and in the world (Clark, 1989)--to assume responsibility for how we are gay, including our sexual and relational behavior. Importantly, Treblicot (1984) further explains that "to take responsibility for [our] sexuality, broadly conceived, is to take responsibility for the whole range of erotic/sexual/gender phenomena that are aspects of [our] actions, attitudes, thoughts, wishes, style and so on" (p. 422).

This emergent demand that we accept responsibility for our actions in the world and with one another--that we synthesize our theological reflection (theory) with all our actions including our sexuality (praxis), in "radical participation" in life here and now (Heyward, 1984, p. 68)--means that gay theological reflection informed by our experience cannot exist in an ethical or moral vacuum. We must, for example, avoid simplistically championing the oppressed-who-can-do-no-wrong (cf., Ruether, 1972, Clark, 1987). In other words, gay liberation theology is necessarily prophetic, claiming and using our position at the very edge of our religious heritage as our standpoint for interpreting and speaking not only from/to our tradition, but also from/ to our own community (cf., Clark, 1989, Morton, 1985). The prophetic demand for justice further means that gay liberation theology and ethics will insist that injustice and homophobia, not (homo)sexuality, draw divine judgment; will accept and affirm that our gay/lesbian sexuality is good a priori; and, will then move on to examine how we may best be and act sexually and in relationship, as gay/lesbian people. To speak prophetically/critically/compassionately to issues of how we are gay, and even how we are sexually and relationally gay, is to seek justice and to seek to make just our sexual behavior and our interpersonal relationships. It is to affirm that gay theology must speak prophetically to represent the "power of freedom and newness of life in which God's word breaks in to speak in judgment on established modes of life and to open up new possibilities" (Ruether, 1985, p. 175, emphasis added, cf., Clark, 1989).

To align ourselves with our divinely intended new possibilities means that just as our theological reflection cannot exist in an ethical vacuum, neither can our actions and our sexuality exist without theological/ethical reflection. That is the dilemma, the problem discovered, which confronts us at the outset of pilgrimaging toward celebration. Nelson (1978) articulately describes the dilemma, as it awaits gay-affirmative theological examination:

> In making moral evaluations of various sexual possibilities both for ourselves and in regard to others, <u>neither moralism nor sentimentalism are helpful</u>. When [sex] becomes compulsive, when a person organizes his or her life around a partial principal, that person pays a heavy cost and the hungered-for communion and integration do not appear. But then <u>moralistic exclusion</u> . . . only <u>compounds the problem</u>. <u>Nor does utter relativism help</u>. (p. 178, emphases added)

He goes on to insist that, while avoiding relativism, ethical reflection should not be addressed to specific <u>acts</u> but rather to the issue of our <u>accountability</u> for the effects of our actions upon ourselves and upon our relationships:

> The more appropriate questions . . . ask about the nature and quality of personal communication which are intended in a sexual act, the kind of communion which that act actually serves, and how all of this fits into the social fabric. (pp. 105-106)

To transpose Nelson's (1978) concern for the "responsible expression" of gay/lesbian sexuality (p. 206) into our specifically gay-affirmative reflections requires confronting certain myths about and false dilemmas imposed upon our sexual behavior. Among common myths, for example, are (from a heterosexist perspective) that gay men, at least, are largely promiscuous and unable to sustain relationships, and (from a gay liberationist perspective) that any efforts to construct an ethical framework for gay/lesbian sexuality will ultimately imitate imperfect heterosexual models and thereby only reinforce internalized homophobia. Confronting and rejecting these myths can enable us to realize that to genuinely affirm our sexuality need <u>not</u> mean accepting "anything goes," as if gay/lesbian sex was really outside the moral order; gay/lesbian love

and sexuality can in fact have an ethically sound un-
derpinning, patriarchal moral codes notwithstanding.
Similarly, to undertake gay self-reflection and even
self-criticism--to refuse to endorse and embrace every-
thing in gay and lesbian life--need not be seen as always anti-gay or as always motivated by some unacknow-
ledged and/or unresolved, internalized homophobia.
Such accusations function as "red herrings" which distract us from the genuinely liberational realization
that total gay self-acceptance and some prophetic/ethi-
cal guidelines and practical limits are not mutually
exclusive. Our call to responsibility and our (com)-
passion for ourselves and our community require that we
make moral decisions and that we do so nonjudgmentally
(or, nonmoralistically) and empathetically. Again,
Heyward (1984) elaborates:

> Compassion and judgment go hand in hand.
> . . . A person who is truly compassionate, truly
> with humanity as friend and advocate, is not timid
> in taking stands which, implicitly or explicitly,
> carry judgment about what is right and wrong, just
> and unjust, acceptable and unacceptable behavior.
> . . . A compassionate person . . . is [also] some-
> one who realizes the bond, the commonness, between
> [him/]herself and those whose actions or attitudes
> [he/]she challenges, criticizes or condemns. (p.
> 239, emphases added)

It is possible to combine--to synthesize--compassion,
empathy, and critical perspective and to embody acceptance and nurturance toward those about whom we care
deeply, even when we disagree fundamentally, and at the
same time to stand under judgment ourselves (cf., Heyward, 1984). That the theologian seeking to discern
appropriate and just ways of acting and relating in the
world also subjects him/herself to the reproval and
redirection inherent in his/her discoveries along the
way is another part of the personal problem-solving dimension of ethical reflection implicit in Nelson's
(1978) introductory remarks.
    To undertake such a pilgrimage as a gay or lesbian
theologian, therefore, also includes looking for some
ethically sound middle ground which reproves and rejects those false dilemmas, which rejects our being
compelled either to enact a reckless promiscuity or to
imitate heterosexual models of monogamy. Just as the
latter is a patriarchal construction, so, too, is gay
promiscuity. As long as we accept patriarchy's devalu-

ation of human sexuality in general, and of our gay/
lesbian sexuality in particular, and as long as we act
in ways which "they" consequently expect us to, those
who enforce patriarchy's hierarchies of exclusion will
continue to have us right where they want us--soul-
lessly marginalized, worthy of moral and religious con-
demnation, and somehow even responsible for AIDS
("blaming the victim"). And yet, clearly, affirming an
ethically responsible gay/lesbian sexuality must not
simplistically imitate heterosexual models. Hetero-
monogamy can also be entrapping and current divorce
rates certainly indicate its failure. There must be,
instead, some middle ground between sexually compulsive
acting-out in our ghettos and disappearing into the
suburbs with our lovers, disengaged from our subculture
and avoiding sexual threats to our seemingly fragile
relationships. Such fearful disengagement and distrust
of our uncoupled peers only betrays our acceptance of
patriarchy's image of us as promiscuous and unable to
sustain meaningful relationship(s).

The tasks which confront our theological and ethical reflection, therefore, are to take responsibility
for (re)constructing our sexuality in fresh ways--God's
new possibilities--and to discern ways of entering into
and sustaining relationships, while also remaining
deeply invested in our subculture and in our community,
as it both yearns for justice and celebrates our sexuality and our relationships. We must explore the possibilities of moving away from double standards of gay
male sexuality vs. lesbian sexuality, and even of appropriate heterosexual sexuality vs. gay sexuality
(cf., Uhrig, 1984), while simultaneously realizing that
our gay/lesbian freedom from certain procreative and
familial concerns should be understood as an opportunity, not as mere license. Nelson (1978) elaborates,
even suggesting a bottom line criterion for our consideration:

> Gay persons desire and need deep and lasting rela-
> tionships just as do heterosexuals, and appropri-
> ate genital expression should be denied to
> neither.
> . . . The ethical question . . . is this:
> what sexual behavior will serve and enhance,
> rather than inhibit, damage, or destroy the fuller
> realization of our divinely-intended humanity?
> The answer is sexual behavior in accord with an
> ethics of love . . . commitment and trust, tender-
> ness, respect for the other, and the desire for

ongoing and responsible communion with the other.
On the negative side, an ethics of love mandates
against selfish sexual expression, cruelty, impersonal sex, obsession with sex, and . . . actions
done without [taking] responsibility for the consequences. Such an ethics always asks about the
meanings of acts in their total context--in the
relationship itself, in society, and in regard to
God's intended direction for human life. Such an
ethics of sexual love is equally appropriate to
heterosexual and gay [people]. There is no double
standard. (pp. 198-199, emphasis added)

A bottom line criterion of love (cf., McNeill, 1988)--
or as Heyward (1982, 1984) reminds us, love in actions
and not merely in eroto-romantic feelings, which is to
say love as the demand for justice--may indeed be our
best guide for discerning the elusive "how" which lures
us into further exploration and reflection. Thus, the
pilgrimage awaits the sorting and gathering of baggage
to set off toward celebration.

These various methodological concerns and resources constitute my own means for sorting baggage and
presuppositions, for laying out my particularity to em-
bark on these theological reflections. These reflections will indeed be phenomenological and confessional:
More than a decade since "coming out," I am still
wrestling with my own "unresolved inner conflict(s)"
about my/our gay sexuality and seeking herein to
achieve some resolution (cf., Nelson, 1978). Moreover,
I believe drawing upon personal experience and developing personal understandings on these issues in dialogue, communicating the "inner world" of my process
(cf., Rubenstein, 1966), can be of some value to
others, insofar as I also believe my dilemmas and concerns are shared and are not merely idiosyncratic. And
thus I bring my relationships, their gifts and their
problems into my reflections--the conflicts between
promiscuity, nonmonogamy, and monogamy; the discrepan-
cies between emotional neediness and independence; the
developmental dilemmas regarding sexual needs and fulfillment; the confusion of celebrating masculinity
while also trying to avoid patriarchal roles and sexist
attitudes and behaviors; the erotic curiosity of
leather somehow unclearly distinct from S/M; and, the
added confusion and grief of "safe sex" and AIDS. Of
course, so much baggage for the journey clearly reminds
me that my concerns and even my tentative solutions
are/will be partial and revisable, and, therefore, any-

thing but authoritative or universal (cf., Heyward, 1984). They remain an invitation to dialogue and are not intended to exclude: Because I acknowledge that I am a white, southern, urban gay male in my mid-thirties, I realize that I certainly cannot speak to or for everybody and that I need and want to hear voices different from my own on these issues.

The limitations of my particularity further compel me to find some grounding and qualification (cf., Ruether, 1983a), and yet my awareness of our gay/lesbian exclusion from the obvious Judaeo-Christian tradition means I will need a variety of sometimes disparate sources in dialogue, qualifying one another as I work my way through their insights. I will consequently be attempting to synthesize gay-sensitive and lesbian/feminist theologians with secular gay liberationist writers; to synthesize general theological and theoretical reflections with the particulars of experience as those have been collected in the data of sociological studies of gay and lesbian couples; to synthesize all of this material with my own sexual interactions and observations; to synthesize critical perspective/ethical guidelines with unabashed celebration; and ultimately/ideally, to synthesize my own sexuality and spirituality with love-as-justice.

My own bottom line is to affirm and to sanctify our gay/lesbian being and our sexuality as the good gifts I know they are and, therefore, to seek our fullest humanity in all its dimensions (cf., Boyd, 1987). I want to engage in a tender, compassionate, empathetic, and searching self-criticism which is open to new possibilities and which, yes, makes judgments for my own life, to make my life whole and to make my relationships just. . . . And, simply, to share that process in order to hear still other voices. The process will entail examining the meaning and potential of human sexuality, as well as the patriarchal stumbling blocks and, specifically, the male socialization process, all of which complicate sexual wholeness, particularly for gay men. It will include wrestling with monogamy/non-monogamy and the related issues of jealousy, envy, and self-esteem, as well as trying to discern the value of certain guidelines and the meaning of the often unclear concept of fidelity, as a broad issue. It will explore traditional and/or accepted models for relationships and envision alternatives and even attempt to understand leather and S/M more clearly, because all the variety of our sexuality deserves reflective attention and, in some form or other,

all this variety also deserves celebration.   With so
much before us, then, let the pilgrimage begin!

*   *   *

II. Human Sexuality and Patriarchal Socialization

(i) (Re)defining and (Re)valuing Human Sexuality

Coming out of the closet to accept and identify oneself as a gay man or lesbian does not necessarily mean that an individual has resolved all of his or her problems and issues about human sexuality in general, or about gay/lesbian sexuality specifically. After all, even the most openly and self-acceptingly gay among us were first enculturated into a puritanical and sex-negative society. As a result, our gay/lesbian sexual relationships and our particular sexual activities are often shaped and restrained not by our mind/body's capacities for pleasure, love, and self-giving interpersonal relationship, but rather by our qualms about sexuality itself, as well as by our lingering guilt about our homosexuality (Clark, 1989). Especially in the face of AIDS and conservative AIDS-phobic pronouncements, we find affirming sexuality and/or bodiliness (our physical limits and mortality) very difficult (cf., Fortunato, 1987, McNeill, 1988). For many gay men, at least, unresolved conflicts over such sexual guilt have lead us to depersonalize our sexuality--both our genitalia and our sexual behavior--and to reduce the whole business to that of a "mere bodily function," as if by severing our sexuality from our sense of self and our spiritual dimensions, we could somehow allay our sexual guilt and continue to act out our sexuality, personally unscathed.

What is most disturbing about this dilemma is that our fear of our bodies, our distrust of the full range of our sexual capacities, and our depersonalization/despiritualization of our sexuality, altogether connect us with the most homophobic of persons. Heyward (1984) pointedly says, for example, that "homophobia is rooted in a fear of the body" (p. 143); moreover,

> . . . for a man to touch and love another man's body is intolerable within the sociotheological walls of an ideology constructed on the def-

inition of a man as a disembodied, rational mind/
spirit that is ever in control and always "above"
body. Thus as a sociopolitical institution, male
homosexuality . . . threatens to bring down the
sacred canopy of an economic, sexual, and racial
order founded on the assumption that the "real
man" is a disembodied, dispassionate agency of
control. . . . [Consequently], gay men who experience, and choose to celebrate, the value of their
bodies and those of other men have a remarkable
opportunity to join in the reshaping of a radically incarnational faith. (pp. 198-199)

Our gay/lesbian sexuality and bodiliness allow us such
a radical opportunity because God in godself is not
homophobic; God created, sanctified, and continues to
celebrate the entire spectrum of human sexuality
(Clark, 1989). Rubenstein (1966) insists, therefore,
that human sin does not lie in our fundamental/original
bodiliness or sexuality, but rather in the prideful refusal of passion, in the embarrassed estrangement from
nature, and in the guilt-ridden spirituality which de-
stroys pleasure and drives people to excess. He
writes, "Only hubris is man's [sic.] real sin [which]
characterizes [our] refusal of the ecstasy and power of
existence. . . . Hubris characterizes [our] refusal of
[our] limits . . . [our] sin against [our] own being,
[our] pathetic refusal to recognize and be [ourselves]"
(p. 137).
    Gay men and lesbians are, absolutely, a part of
God's good creation and our capacities for sexual love
are absolutely not sinful. In fact, our various sexual
differences, "like other signs of uniqueness in our
lives, need to be celebrated, not castigated," as part
of God's own delight in the plurality and variety of
creation (Boyd, 1984, p. 129). McNeill (1987) similarly elaborates:

    God so created humans that they develop with a
    great variety of both gender identities and sexual
    object choices. . . . Homosexuals or lesbians
    . . . should be considered as part of God's crea-
    tive plan. Their sexual orientation . . . is a
    gift from God to be accepted and lived out with
    gratitude. God does not despise anything that God
    has created. (p. 243)

He goes on to contend that not only does every human
being have a "God-given right to sexual love and inti-

macy" (p. 243), but that "only a sadistic God would create hundreds of thousands of humans to be inherently homosexual and then deny them the right to sexual intimacy" (p. 244, cf., Barrett, 1978). Denying our loving sexuality is clearly not required of us; God created all human sexuality and God sanctifies all responsible, caring, loving, mutually pleasuring sexuality (Clark, 1989).

The way out of our puritanical sex-negativity--the means for overcoming our learned estrangement from earth/nature/cycles/limits--may in fact lie in our ability to revalue and resanctify both our bodiliness and our sexuality, in our ability to transform the profane into the sacred by sanctifying the "physical/sexual" (cf., Satloff, 1983, p. 202). Revaluing our sexuality as wholeness-making and loving can thus (re)connect us to God's love for all creation and can thus in turn enable us to revalue our gay/lesbian selves. If (homo)sexual sin/guilt no longer has power over us, then we are free to celebrate both our sexuality and our gay self-worth as equally gifts from God (cf., Boyd, 1984). Such a radical reaffirmation of all human sexuality and especially gay/lesbian sexuality has never been as important as now, before the spectres of AIDS and AIDS-phobically strengthened sex-negativity and homophobia (Clark, 1989).

As lesbians and gay men, in particular, we must absolutely refuse to allow AIDS to destroy our sexual energy or our sacramental capacities for loving mutuality, borne in and nurtured by our particular sexuality. Instead, we must responsibly and consistently adopt, and adapt to, "safe-sex" practices (cf., Appendix A), while insisting still upon the sexual/spiritual interconnectedness and empowerment we experience in our sexually deepened relationships. Our loving one another now, even more deeply and passionately (and safely), can in fact strengthen our mutuality in community and our shared, caring response to those who suffer with AIDS, while also informing our every effort against homophobia and for our liberation (Clark, 1989). And yet, to make such a radical affirmation of our bodiliness and our sexuality in these times will not be an easy task. Our gay theological and ethical reflections must therefore enable us to redefine and reunderstand our sexuality in ways which reveal its liberational potential for our lives.

To begin such a redefining of sexuality means we must immediately relinquish the notion that sexual behavior is merely a bodily function, some impersonal act external to who we are. Indeed, our sexuality does not just entail "something we do; it is an inalienable dimension of what we are" (McNeill, 1988, p. 123). Silverstein (1981), for example, acknowledges that "sex is not characterized by its conclusion, the orgasm," among the gay male couples he studied; rather, "it is a complex interaction, a system of communication between two or more people" (p. 194). Human sexuality is just too complex for a simplistic reduction to bodily/genital function alone. Thus, Silverstein (1981) further suggests that "people experience different kinds of bodily and psychological [and spiritual] needs at different times, perhaps with different experiences mixed together under the rubric of the sexual" (p. 336, emphasis added). Nelson (1978) anticipates Silverstein's (1981) research conclusions when he also emphasizes both the complexity and the interpersonal communication inherent in our sexuality. He suggests that our sexuality depends upon socially constructed patterns of meaning and that sexual behavior includes both our need for, and a symbolic means to, communication and communion. As a yearning toward communion with another, our sexuality "expresses God's intention that we find our authentic humanness in relation" (p. 18) and, hence, "sexuality appears to be intrinsically . . . related to one's capacity to love" (p. 75). Moreover, because "our embodied sexuality is the physiological and psychological base for our capacity to love" (p. 198), Nelson (1978) adamantly refuses to separate sex from love, from the human need for meaningful relationship. He even goes so far as to contend that the most promiscuous behavior is driven, at some subliminal level, by this need for loving relationship:

> The actions of even the most wildly promiscuous individual are remnants of a residual health: they are the restless cries for embodied love, needing more than . . . condemnation--needing healing of the wounds of emotional and spiritual deprivation and release from the tyrannies of exploitive behavior. (p. 157, cf., p. 86, cf., McNeill, 1988)

Not unlike gay St. Aelred some eight centuries earlier, Nelson (1978) goes on to insist that the urge for communion, expressed through loving sexual fulfillment, even discloses God to us.[2] Our sexuality is also "intrinsic to our relationship with God" (p. 18) and the communion we find in sexual love includes genuine divine presence (Clark, 1987, 1989). McNeill (1988) even goes so far as to suggest that "there is a sensuous and even erotic dimension to our love of God" (p. 123). Our sexuality and our spirituality, our deepest selfhood, are thus absolutely inseparable. Lesbian/feminist theologian, Heyward (1984), has expanded on this broader reconceptualization of sexuality as our urge toward relationship with other persons and with God and, thus, as simultaneously socially and spiritually sacramental:

> The yearning within me for meaningful relationship to help me validate my own being is, in fact, simultaneously a sexual and a spiritual yearning for relationship and . . . this yearning is not only good, but that which brings me to life, to risk, to courage, to commitment, to passion, to vocation, to feelings, to sisters and brothers, and, yes, to God.
>
> . . . The integrity in which spirituality and sexuality are realized as one flow of being, relating us both to God and to sisters and brothers, enables self-validation. It is God with us. (pp. 44-45)

For us as gay men and lesbians, gay self-acceptance and liberation does not depend upon our alienation from our sexual behavior, or upon our capacity to separate our deepest selfhood from our genital function. Our capacity for the deepest and truest self-acceptance lies, instead, in our ability to reconceptualize our sexuality as the sacred urge in us for relationship with one another; that same unyielding urge and that deep self-acceptance also disclose God to us.

Moreover, as we are able to reintegrate our genital sexual expression, our desire for meaningful relationship, and our spirituality as a unity, a wholeness, we begin to realize the broader liberational empowerment of our sexuality. Because our sexual yearnings urge us toward loving relationship, that desire for compassionate right-relationship opens us to a desire for justice in all relationships. Sex, love, and justice are inextricably connected, as Heyward (1984) again elaborates:

> Our sexuality is our desire to participate in making love, making justice, in the world; our drive toward one another; our movement in love; our ex-

pression of our sense of being bonded together in
life and death.
    . . . Where there is no justice . . . there
is no love. And where there is no justice/no
love, sexuality is perverted into violence and vi-
olation, the effects of which most surely include
. . . emotional . . . battering, [manipulation/
control], competition and contempt.
    . . . The ecstatic power of the sex act can
lead us to identify it wrongly with the whole of
sexuality, when in truth sexuality is, I believe,
the one most vital source of our other passions,
of our capacities to love and to do what is just
in the world. . . . To celebrate sexuality is
linked inextricably with the capacity to court
peace, instead of war; justice, instead of oppression; life, instead of hunger, torture, fear,
crime, and death. (pp. 86, 78)

Our sexuality is absolutely not merely some bodily
function crying for release; in fact, our sexuality-as-
gift is the complex psycho-spiritual and physical nexus
of our capacities for love and meaningful, just relationship (cf., Nelson, 1978). Most importantly for us
as a marginalized gay and lesbian people, our complex
sexuality is the very foundation and well-spring of our
unrelenting demand for justice. Our sexuality as an
urge for right-relationship, for justice, is itself our
very source of empowerment for the tasks of liberation,
for our quests for justice for ourselves and for
others.
    Just as Heyward (1984) can, therefore, insist that
"love is full of such yearning, such adamant insistence
for right-relation, such compassion [agape]" (p. 88),
so the scholar of gay-related biblical passages, Edwards (1984), similarly insists that agapeic love "morally informs human sexuality" and gives to sexuality
its broader, liberational potential (p. 107). Without
devaluing the importance of genital expression, Edwards
(1984) also seeks to avoid and to transcend sexual acts
reductionism; like Heyward (1984), he synthesizes our
sexuality with our broader liberation struggle:

    Transgenital awareness attempts to place sexuality
in appropriate relationship to the total moral
task of liberating love . . . establishing person-
hood beyond the confines of sexual functions.
    . . . Sexual love is paradoxical in its abi-
lity to express self-centered, instinctive, and

immediate gratification, on the one hand, and powerful self-giving on the other. The moral task of
theology is to exemplify and teach the fulfilling
of sexual love [as] the basis for a mutuality that
no longer seeks surrender and self-sacrifice from
the other, pleasure and domination for the self.
(pp. 123, 111)

Both Heyward (1984) and Edwards (1984) are concerned that our failure to transcend patriarchy's op-
pressive genital function reductionism--our frequent
inability to synthesize our sexuality with the totality
of our being--lies in our inability to live within the
paradox Edwards (1984) describes. As a result, we use
our alienated sexual activity-as-release to protect
ourselves from intimacy and to keep people at a dis-
tance--despite the physical closeness required for or-
gasm--rather than incorporating our sexuality-as-gift
into our deepest expressions of/needs for intimacy and
our most profound commitments to justice and right relation. Says Heyward (1984),

. . . The immorality in relationship results
primarily from a fear of [real intimacy]; the inability to make commitment; to be vulnerable to
another; to be honest . . .; to sustain interest
in loving relationship . . .; or to realize actively that loving does indeed involve fear and
loss and [even] death. (p. 48)

Nelson (1978) has similarly described this dilemma.
While he, too, realizes that "our sexuality is . . .
part of what it means to be human, [that] it is a power
to be integrated fully into one's self-hood and to be
used in the service of love" (p. 188), he also concedes
both the idealism of his vision of sexual wholeness and
the reality of our frequent inability to live in the
paradox, when he earlier says, "Even at those times
when we refuse to affirm it we are capable of affirming
this: sex is intended to be a language of love" (p.
109).
       Our capacity to reconceptualize our sexuality as
both a physical need and a psycho-spiritual urge into
just and loving interpersonal relationships--to redefine our sexuality as both a genital expression and the
transgenital source of our empowerment for liberation--
remains an ideal before us which is very difficult to
reach, to make real, to realize. As a result, Marcus'
(1988) recent study of gay male couples reflects both

the complexity Silverstein (1981) discovered earlier
and the real frustration, even brokenness, underlying
the concerns of Nelson (1978), Edwards (1984), and Heyward (1984). Marcus (1988) concludes,

> . . . Sex is physical need, affection, affir-
> mation of attractiveness and desirability. It can
> be an expression of love and it can also be excit-
> ing, pleasurable, and a lot of fun. But sex can
> also be the source of anger, tension, competition,
> anxiety, and jealousy. (p. 135)

Our reconceptualization of our sexuality as something
complex, whole, and integral to our very being as
people, and as gay and lesbian people, is frustrated by
the dualistic force of paradox. Before we can live
within paradox, within a creative tension begetting
unity and wholeness, we must examine the dualisms which
patriarchy and particularly the male socialization process have bequeathed to us. These dualisms and their
influence upon us are among the most difficult stumbling blocks we must face en route to the realization
and celebration of our vision of genuinely liberated
sexual wholeness and empowerment.

(ii) Deconstructing Patriarchal Dualisms
and Male Socialization

The patriarchal structures, against which we must
struggle together to revalue our sexuality, are deeply
embedded in our society and culture, as well as in our
western religious heritage. In fact, the inordinate
valuing of heterosexual men and their procreative sexuality (heterosexism) entered western consciousness simultaneously with the very beginning of the Judaeo-
Christian tradition. As Bauman (1983) sardonically remarks, "Attributing sanctity to male gender and phallus
initiate[d] the whole saga of the Jewish people with
Abraham's everlasting covenant with his god through a
mark on his penis" (p. 91). What began with Abraham
and the patriarchs of Judaism influenced Christianity,
which in turn influenced all subsequent western consciousness. Ultimately, the human need for "ontological security," the progression of patriarchal duality
toward structured meaning, developed as a need to control, especially to control sexuality and human interrelationships (cf., Walker, 1980). Within Christianity
it produced an ascetic spirituality utterly opposed to
the body-affirming doctrine of creation (Collins, 1974,

Ruether, 1972, cf., Fortunato, 1987). This persistent mind/body or spirit/body dualism in Christianity was not a novel concept, however. Christianity simply infused already dualistic Greek ideas with a parallel set of concepts implicit in first century Judaism between the sacred or spiritual realm (ruhniut) and the profane world of the physical, of bodiliness (gashmiut); this dualism, which influenced all subsequent western culture and thought, both reflected and shaped a need to regulate and control unruly sexuality "because of its threat to the sexuality of men" (Plaskow, 1983, p. 225).

Finding its fullest expression in Christianity, this polarization of the "self" or the spirit from the world and the body easily led to the polarization of the "self" from other persons. The accompanying hierarchical values clearly placed heterosexual, ascetic (or, sexless) men over against both women and homosexuals, who were more associated with sexuality, the passions, and the irrational. Private, individual sexuality became the heart of religious doctrines of sin and salvation, while social injustice and social reformation were ignored by the status quo (Ruether, 1972).

Ironically, patriarchy's disproportionate devaluation of human sexuality not only led it to externalize, objectivize, and empty sexuality of spiritual meaning; it also led western culture, and particularly Christianity, to become obsessed with the very sexuality it sought to stifle (cf., Clark, 1989). The narrow categorization of people and behaviors which has resulted, the restrictions and either/ors of rigid gender roles and sexual behavior roles (hetero- vs. homosexuality, for example), has diminished all human sexuality and undermined the fecund energies which nurture human relationships and which motivate human love and justice, the very stuff of humane existence (cf., Heyward, 1984). Moreover, by making sexuality sinful, and by further confining sexuality to rigid gender roles and reducing its appropriate place solely to that of procreation, patriarchy also severed sexuality from intimate human loving: "Our society has not cultivated in us the capacity to link sexuality and love, to relate caring for another to physical attraction to that person" (Doustourian, 1978, p. 335). Patriarchal/procreative sexuality ignores the relationally enhancing power of sexuality as the expression of love and mutuality in relationships. It fails to acknowledge the possibility that human sexuality, as loving, pleasuring, humanizing, and empowering, is _intrinsically_ valuable (cf., Doustourian, 1978, Heyward, 1984, Clark, 1989).

While Silverstein (1981) extends the _intrinsic_ (re)valuation of sexuality to the extent of arguing that the persistent need to qualify all sexual behavior with "love and mutuality" is itself patriarchally anti-sexual, Nelson (1978) is more concerned that the failure to do so simply reinforces mind/body and love/sex dualisms, resulting in quests for "orgasmic experience divorced from the integrity of the person" (p. 66). Similarly, Fortunato (1987) is concerned with our ongoing alienation from our embodiment, our continuing inability to reunite/reintegrate selfhood and bodiliness and/or our capacity for love and our sexuality:

> At a subliminal level . . . many of us still feel . . . that it is somehow holier (purer) to be non-sexual; holier (more selfless) to pass up worldly pleasures than to enjoy them; holier (humbler) to deny oneself and submit to someone else--anyone else--than to exercise one's free will. . . . We remain a schizophrenic culture, constantly battling some deep-seated sense of shame about what our bodies are and what they do. (p. 58)

Ultimately, our continuing sexual shame and not any efforts to qualify/control sexuality with "love and mutuality" keeps us alienated from our bodiliness and from the humanizing and empowering potential of an integrated sexuality and spirituality. Consequently, McNeill (1988) has suggested that "the most profound and most frequent sin concerning our bodies . . . has nothing to do with sexual activity. . . . It has to do with our alienation from our body and its sexual feelings" (p. 214). Nelson (1978) even argues that such alienation leads us not toward the (re)valuation of sexuality free from any qualification or control, which Silverstein (1981) suggests, but rather toward the continued devaluation of our bodies and our genitalia as mere machines:

> The sense of body as machine . . . is the phenomenon experienced by both the ascetic and the libertine. . . . The ascetic experiences the body as a dangerous, alien force to be sternly controlled, even crushed into submission. It is "the lower realm," whose experiences cannot be integrated into the moral self. For the libertine, the body becomes the instrument of sensuality. It is dri-

ven in a restless pursuit of pleasure. It is detached from the ego's vulnerability and capacity for self-surrender. Rather, it becomes an instrument, . . . a tool which wards off love. . . .

The problem of this dualistic alienation is further complicated by the fact that an oppressed or rejected body (whether for reasons of the ascetic within us or the libertine) becomes a nemesis. It seeks its revenge. . . . The body's ghostly influence continues, but in ways little understood by or integrated into the self. Deprived of eros [love], the body can become the champion of thanatos [death]. (pp. 40-41)

This profound concern with our persistent inability to integrate sex and love, as well as with our continuing denigration of our bodies as machines and of our sexuality as "mere bodily functions," has led Evans (1988) to suggest that, for gay men at least, the results of such patriarchal alienation have indeed been deadly. While he stops just short of "blaming the victim," he does contend that the structures of patriarchy which framed a gay male subculture of alienated, despiritualized, and mechanical sexual behavior also created a gay male subculture which has been inordinately vulnerable to sexually transmitted diseases of all kinds, including AIDS. In other words, the gay male community was first a victim of patriarchy's devaluation/externalization/alienation of human sexuality before it also became a victim of thanatos, of a random virus itself blind to sexual orientation and value issues. Because the patriarchal dichotomies of spirituality/sexuality and love/sex have had such an impact upon the gay (male) subculture, our efforts to deconstruct patriarchy's sway over us and to affirm, instead, a redefinition and revaluation of our sexuality further require that we examine not only the development of patriarchal dualisms, but the male socialization process itself which they undergird, and its additional impact on gay male sexuality.

In her early study of gay and lesbian couples, Mendola (1980) noted that gay male sexuality, particularly its seeming aversion to sustained monogamy, was not so much the result of her male interview subjects' being gay, as their being the products of the heterosexist enculturation of all males under patriarchy. Although Silverstein (1981) acknowledged, in his own subsequent yet still pre-AIDS study of gay male couples, that sexuality is "a complex interaction" as

well as "a system of communication" (p. 194) and that a
variety of experiences actually converge "under the
rubric of the sexual" (p. 336), he also reduced all
male sexuality to a simplistic combination of essentially two drives: physical genital satisfaction and a
physiologically based need for excitement (p. 332).
More importantly, Silverstein (1981) also adamantly de-
fended patriarchally shaped male sexuality as appropriate for gay men, over against charges by feminists and
some gay liberationists. He says at length,

> . . . Men [gay or non-gay] seem to like vari-
> ety and change, enjoy the opportunity for moments
> of tenderness as well as rough sexual play with an
> unknown person without the desire to continue
> [the] relationship. Experienced men are excep-
> tionally competent in distinguishing between the
> act of sex and the commitment of love . . .
> (though such "objectification" is deplored by many
> gay liberationists and feminists).
> . . . Most men adore being sex objects; they
> like the idea of using each other's bodies as ob-
> jects of physical pleasure on a temporary basis
> and have no difficulty separating this from their
> needs for love [because] at other times, nurtur-
> ance and comfort are part of . . . sex. . . .
> These [various] actions seem to be legitimate ways
> for men to express their physical sexual needs.
> . . . To suggest that there is anything intrinsi-
> cally bad about free and frequent expression with
> only the goal of the utmost physical pleasure
> seems to be once again a historic fear of and
> anger at human sexuality. (pp. 330-331)

He goes on to say that gay male sexuality need not
be interpreted or judged either by heterosexual models
or by the historical experience of women with heterosexual men:

> There is no reason to believe that men's sexual
> diversity is oppressive to anyone, and gay men
> should feel free to express themselves with com-
> patible partners. It is also historically quaint
> to think of male sexuality as "promiscuous." . . .
> [The term's] use today seems motivated by those
> who either fear sexuality or are jealous of an-
> other's pleasure. (p. 336)

Ironically, Silverstein's (1981) admirable efforts to describe the realities of (gay) male sexuality before AIDS and, therein, to avoid both anti-sexualism and the simplistic imitation of heterosexual models and, further, to revalue sexuality in itself, are deflected by his own rootedness in patriarchy. He endorses dichotomizing love and sex, as well as treating one's body and one's sexual partners as objects or "machines" (cf., Nelson, 1978). His efforts to revalue sexuality only reflect the patriarchal alienation which shaped a gay (male) subculture of unreflective "sexual diversity" in the years prior to AIDS.

The patriarchal male socialization which entrapped Silverstein (1981) still haunts gay male relationships today, as more recent studies indicate. For example, while Reece and Segrist (1988) imply that male socialization need not negatively affect gay male couplings--that masculine identified partners may actually be more cooperative than more androgynous men--Peplau and Cochran (1988) concede not only that male socialization encourages gay men to separate sexuality from love and emotional intimacy, but that the gay male subculture still reinforces this dichotomy. Similarly, when McWhirter and Mattison (1984) describe western, patriarchally enculturated men, gay or non-gay, as goal-oriented, conflict- and adventure-seeking, competitive, aggressive, and emotionally controlled, they admit that the "obvious potential for clash, competition, and dissonance is very high" when two gay men shaped by such enculturation attempt a relationship (p. 130). In other words, two competitively socialized gay men may find building a cooperative, long term relationship very difficult. In the most recent gay/lesbian couples study, Berzon (1988) even goes so far as to insist that competitive male socialization is actually "antithetical to the most important aspects of successful . . . intimate partnership: the ability to open up and become known to another person, the willingness to be vulnerable to another, the valuing of equality, the commitment to collaborating rather than competing" (p. 119). She later adds that "if two men are unable to break out of their conditioning [to be competitive, unemotional, and uncomfortable with affection and praise], their relationship will not be the source of warmth and emotional nourishment that it might be" (p. 347).

Even Silverstein (1981) ultimately admits that, among more masculinely identified gay men, male socialization breeds possessiveness, competition, envy, and fear of abandonment, all often unconsciously confused and masked as jealousy. Particularly given the post-Stonewall (post-1969) remasculinization of many gay men, various problems in gay male relationships may in fact be complicated by both partner's enculturation as males, "each imbued and trained in the demands of masculinity as defined by our society" (p. 180). In its extreme form, according to Silverstein (1981), "cult masculinity" becomes selfish, aggressive, controlling, and anti-sexual; conquest becomes more important than intimacy or pleasure and "the need for excitement overcomes the need for sensual and genital pleasure" (p. 334). Silverstein (1981) further elaborates:

> Cult masculinity [is] an antisexual movement, even though outwardly it praises and glories in sexual abandon. [Despite the frequency and number of sexual partners], the symbols of masculinity hide real sexual needs. . . . Power, coldness, and competition replace physical sensuousness. . . . This symbolization [is] antithetical to sexual pleasure [or fulfillment] and certainly to the acceptance [sustenance or maintenance] of a love relationship, except of the briefest variety. (p. 329)

Again, Silverstein's (1981) own observations of gay male couples and of the more extreme expressions of male socialization in the gay male community undercut his (re)valuational efforts. Male socialization, coupled with the love/sex dichotomy and alienated sexual behavior, remains problematic, as Nelson (1978) again anticipates: "The masculine orientation to sex tends strongly toward genital-centeredness. . . . This, in turn, nurtures self-conscious, mechanical perspectives about sex and leads to the diminution of capacities for self-giving, tenderness, ecstasy, and play" (p. 67), and, ultimately, toward a need for ever increasing extremes of "play" to enable any "ecstasy." The "pressure to perform" and the focus on specific genital "acts" are ultimately de-eroticizing, leading to an inability to "perform" and to a waning sexual interest between long term partners (Nelson, 1978).

More recently, again, Evans (1988) expresses a similar concern that patriarchal male socialization represses unified "sexual and emotional essentials" and encourages men's needs both to compete and to prove their masculinity, as well as their inability to love (cf., p. 81). He alternately calls this the "patriarchal model of masculinity" (p. 111) and the "patriar-

chal psychosis" (p. 178). Echoing Nelson (1978), he
also criticizes both the sexual objectification and
self-objectification which has resulted among men who
use "their own bodies as disposable objects in the pursuit of orgasms, money, or power" (Evans, 1988, p.
181). Evans (1988) also clearly perceives the extent
to which male socialization's disdain for things feminine reinforces homophobia and undermines gay self-
acceptance. In a particularly acerbic passage, he
turns his critical eye upon the gay male subculture:

> The patriarchal psychosis has also taken its
> toll within gay male relationships, since the
> great majority of American gay men are acutely
> anxiety-ridden about their masculinity, just like
> their heterosexual counterparts. An evidence of
> this anxiety is the extreme lengths to which many
> American gay men now feel they have to go in order
> not to be taken for "sissies." . . . A new gay
> stereotype is being created that is almost a sat-
> ire on masculinity. . . . Among such gay men there
> is often an extreme hostility to feminine-identi-
> fied [or androgynous] men. (pp. 178-179)[3]

More compassionate in their gay self-criticism,
Goodman, et al. (1983), have also recognized the fact
that patriarchy, male socialization, and its attendant
homophobia not only keep sex roles in place, but also
preclude real intimacy between men and women, and especially between men and other men: "Homophobia . . .
helps keep the masculine/feminine dichotomy in place,
which deprives individuals of wholeness and maintains
men's power over women"; moreover, patriarchal male socialization "trains us to believe that safe, caring,
supportive relationships between men are impossible"
(pp. 3, 35). Goodman, et al. (1983), suspect that, ultimately, male socialization makes genuine interpersonal intimacy between gay men very difficult, if not virtually impossible:

> Some of us have trouble accepting the love of
> other men and really believing in it; . . . some
> of us who are gay are cynical about the gay world.
> . . . It's hard for us to meet a new man [and be-
> lieve] that he will like us and will deal gently
> with us. . . . We remain wary. He is, after all,
> a man. (p. 109)

And our wariness about our peers is never stronger than when we come through the process of ending a relationship, somehow sharing both the grief over and the responsibility for our failures to simultaneously sustain intimacy, compassion, and sexual interest/affection. A way out of this dilemma for gay men may lie in just this process of consciousness-raising, of examining and deconstructing patriarchal dualisms and the effects of male socialization. With such a heightened awareness, perhaps we can begin to reclaim our vision and move to embrace a redefinition and resacramentalization of our sexuality which transcends our dilemma and which ultimately leads us toward the reconciliation of dualistic opposites and, thus, toward gay (male) sexual wholeness.

(iii) Reconstructing Gay Sexual Wholeness

During the 1980s a plethora of gay and gay-sensitive writers have both prophetically and compassionately addressed our needs as a gay/lesbian people, both to transcend patriarchy's cruel power over our sexuality and to realize thereby our redefinition and revaluation of gay/lesbian sexuality and, ultimately, of all human sexuality. McNeill (1988), for example, is deeply concerned about the alienation from our bodies and the depersonalization of our sexuality which patriarchal socialization has reinforced among us, particularly within the gay male community. He is consequently aware that the "unloving suppression of the self's erotic needs frequently leads to the destructive acting out of those needs" (p. 125). Heyward (1984) has similarly realized that the "cult of body worship in gay male culture, just as in straight male culture, [is] a structure of sexist/heterosexist oppression" (p. 198). She urges us to relinquish treating others as sexual objects, separating our sexual "acts" from our sense of self, and pursuing genital experience as object or goal. Instead of these behavior patterns, she offers a vision in which selfhood, embodiment, sexuality, and spirituality are one. McNeill (1988) is equally adamant that, in fact, "God intends sexual wholeness" for all gay men and lesbians (p. 125). Hay (1987) even believes that one possible result of the tragic impact of AIDS upon the gay male community in particular may just be to open us to such a wholistic vision:

The catalyst of spiritual crisis . . . has brought many gay men face-to-face with the appalling dichotomy between . . . the nurturing sensitivity and concern for each other in a mutuality of sexual intimacy, that we all profess to be seeking, [and] the desolation and alienation from self and from each other that more often takes place, as we make sexual objects of ourselves and of each other in pursuit of traditional and expected behavior. (p. 288)

Virtually synthesizing Hay's (1987) and McNeill's (1988) concerns with Heyward's (1984) vision of unity, Boyd (1987) says that "our spiritual needs cry out to be met, honestly and fully, integrated with our sexual and other needs" (p. 84). Similarly, Fortunato (1983, 1987) insists that, because both our sexuality and our spirituality are gifts from God, they belong together. Emphasizing the importance of our overcoming the fragmentation of our good gay sexuality from the wholeness of who we are, he concludes that "the mission to which we are called," as gay men and lesbians, is to affirm our "sexual-spiritual wholeness" (1987, p. 33). Most recently, McNeill (1988) has similarly insisted that the "prophetic role" of gay men and lesbians is to lead not only our own community(ies), but all of "western culture toward reembracing embodiment, toward a sense of identity with the body and its sensuousness" (pp. 125-126). He adds that our prophetic task, therefore, is "to integrate [our] sexual nature into our power to love--to love ourselves, to love each other, and ultimately to love God with our whole [spiritual/physical/sexual] being" (p. 127).

Even apart from these gay theological writers, secular gay liberationists and others are also addressing these same issues. Goodman, et al. (1983), for example, have expanded on this concern that we overcome the patriarchal love/sex dichotomy and that we reunify and relearn the wholeness of sensuality, sexuality, and physical affection:

Sexual expression is distorted by [western] culture . . . since the preoccupation is with performance, the genitals, and orgasm.
        . . . Sexuality and sensuality need to merge . . . as affection and touching are recognized as necessary and desirable for human health and sex loses its genital and orgasmic preoccupation.

. . . Orgasm is not the issue; caring is what matters. (pp. 47, 48)

Evans (1988) similarly insists that "the opposite of the patriarchal psychosis is the ability to love" and the opposite of objectification and alienation is the (re)development of genuine compassion and empathy for one another (p. 181). He goes on to say that, instead of continued repressive sex/love and sexual/spiritual alienation, "we need a new definition of what it means to be a human being. To that end, we each need access to the full range of [our sexual and emotional] human capacities," toward a more balanced and whole way of living (p. 192, cf., p. 198). And, once again, non-gay theologian Nelson (1978) has anticipated many of these gay/lesbian concerns as he urges us to exchange alienated body/self and sex/love understandings of sexuality for an affirmation of diffused, whole-body sensuality that can lead us to a recognition of the sensuality in all things (cf., Fortunato, 1987).

Not surprisingly, feminist theologians have long been at the forefront of liberational efforts to dissolve these dualistic separations, particularly the devaluation of bodiliness and sexuality from spirituality and loving mutuality. In so doing, they provide our gay theological and ethical reflections with rich resources to enable us to reclaim and expand our vision of sexuality and, thereby, to approach balance and wholeness as sexual gay/lesbian people (cf., Clark, 1989). In the very face of patriarchy's tyranny over our lives and our sexuality, these writers insist at the outset, up front, that our bodies, our selves, and our spirits are in fact one; we are our embodiedness (cf., Heyward, 1984). Anticipating Evans (1988), for example, Christ (1980) argues that,

. . . Rather than ignoring or denying feelings of connection to nature, women (and others) need to develop a new understanding of being human, in which the body is given a more equal footing with the intellect and the human connection to nature is positively valued at the same time that the awesome (but not unlimited) human capacity to manipulate and control nature is recognized. (p. 129)

Similarly, Heyward (1984) insists that "all liberation theology reveals a bias for the spirituality in physicality, the spirit in flesh, the God in humanity" (p.

173). Ruether (1983a, 1983b) is equally clear in her assertion that the rejection, domination, and exploitation of nature, of other people, and of our bodies are all connected. Dominated people, for example, are always devalued as closer to nature, more bodily and sensual, and less spiritual (i.e., less valuable). Ultimately, she argues that both a "world-fleeing spirituality" and the "fear of embodiment as moral debasement" reflect our fear of death, our refusal to accept our limits (1983a, p. 79, 1983b, p. 61). The clear alternative which feminist theology offers for this dilemma is "an explicit and unequivocal commitment to the liberation of the body [and nature] from disrepute, the liberation of sexuality from contempt and embarrassment, the liberation of feelings from trivialization, and the liberation of death and dying from shame and denial" (Heyward, 1984, p. 174). In short, feminist theology makes a "radically incarnational affirmation" that the body is good and that full (i.e., sexual) participation in bodily existence "is to participate in the movement of divinity" (Heyward, 1984, p. 172).

Outside feminist theology, Rubenstein (1966) has anticipated these same concerns when he admonishes us "to acknowledge our temporality and mortality without illusion" (p. 238), as well as "to learn how to dwell in our bodies. . . . Fewer capacities come harder to Americans," he adds, "than the capacity to dwell in [our] bodies with grace, dignity, and gratification," and without guilt (p. 239). Our gay theological and ethical reflections consequently call us also to affirm, again in the very face of AIDS, both the goodness of our limits or mortality and the absolute sanctity of our bodies and our sexuality (cf., Fortunato, 1987, McNeill, 1988). If we are able to affirm that our bodies, our sexuality, and our spirituality are unitary and good, we can then move to free not only our bodies, but our sexuality as well, from repression (cf., Clark, 1989).

As with dissolving the dualism of body/spirit, our extended efforts to break down the related dualism of sexuality/spirituality, and thus to free our repressed and marginalized sexualities, can also begin in the insights and analyses of feminist theology (Clark, 1989). Heyward (1984), for example, simply rejects a dualistic theological tradition which separates sacred and profane, spirit and body, a god "up there" and human embodiment "down here." She insists, instead, upon the integrity of our spirituality and our sexuality as "one flow of being" (p. 45). She also urges us to eroticize agape and to synthesize sexual and spiritual love, insisting that "the command to love neighbor as self has as much to do with eros and philia as with agape" (p. 90). Numerous gay religious writers have extended and/or elaborated this feminist message that to affirm bodiliness also entails affirming sexuality and that bodiliness, sexuality, and spirituality are all one (cf., Clark, 1989). Boyd (1984), for example, insists that the "sacred and the secular are truly knit together" whenever we make sexual love "in the sincere hope of sharing communion" (pp. 140, 144).

Both Uhrig (1984) and Edwards (1984) also echo feminist concerns when they reiterate the fact that the sexuality/spirituality dualism has not only distorted sexual love as sinful, but has actually alienated gay men and lesbians from our inherent spiritual capacities, because we are seen (and we too often see ourselves) as only sexual. Defiantly rejecting the schism of sexuality/spirituality in an effort to heal its resultant alienation, Uhrig (1984) argues that our gay/lesbian sexuality is actually the very locus of our encounter with divine acceptance and empowerment: "Lesbians and gay men now have a prophetic function to fulfill. . . . Consistent with the [fact] that God always chooses a rejected people through whom to act, gay people are revealing the reunion of sexuality and spirituality" (p. 80); moreover, "our essential task is to unify spirituality and sexuality, and to embody this union in our lives and relationships" (p. 106). Our gay theological and ethical reflections, then, must not fail to include our opportunity, and our responsibility, to advocate and to embody a conciliatory return to divinely intended sexual/spiritual integration and wholeness, as well as to both reconceptualize and reunderstand that sexuality is a means to communion with God by way of communion with another person (cf., Clark, 1989, McNeill, 1988, Uhrig, 1984). As we are able to dissolve and reconcile the dualisms of body/spirit and sexuality/spirituality, we may also be able to discover that God is with us in our sexuality and that, consequently, our sexuality is the very ground of both our spiritual and our sociopolitical power. We may even be able to set aside our limited and limiting understandings of sex as either sinful or mechanical and, instead, embrace our broadened and resanctified understanding of sexuality in all its liberational potential (Clark, 1989).

Numerous gay/lesbian writers have already begun this reclaiming and resanctifying process as they advocate freeing sexuality from the confines of either utilitarian procreation or rigid gender roles. Freed from function, role, and even mere orgasm, our sexuality can instead be our mutual and egalitarian means for rediscovering playful and compassionate intimacy and for reestablishing the importance of love in our relationships (cf., Edwards, 1984, Fox, 1983, Goodman, et al., 1983, McNeill, 1988). Apart from procreative roles and functions, for example, the open, active, unfettered sexuality of gay men and lesbians "may be the means for us to finally learn to go beyond orgasm to much deeper levels of intimacy," thereby allowing us the freedom to enjoy "varied levels of intimacy and . . . intensities of relationship" (Uhrig, 1984, p. 82). Similarly, McNeill (1987) writes that "what is unique to human sexuality is the fusion that God has made of biological sexuality with the uniquely human vocation to, and capacity for, love" (p. 245, cf. McNeill, 1988). While the anti-sexual biases or pervasive sex-negativity of western consciousness have repressed our bio-erotic need for intimacy and relationship, leading to brokenness, alienation, injustice, and exploitation, our sexuality as a drive toward relationship and mutuality with one another, and with the divine in turn, may actually be the "most important reality we have" (cf., Rubenstein, 1966, p. 78).

This same radical affirmation of sexuality is taken up and extended most adamantly by Heyward (1984). Her radically participatory liberation theology links sexual enspiritment and empowerment with social action. Sexuality is an extension, a deepening, and an expression of both human intimacy and our commitments to action. As our drive toward loving human interrelationship, our marginalized gay/lesbian sexuality becomes the very ground and empowering source for our efforts to make justice and to effect liberation in this world, here and now. Not only is sexuality "the undercurrent of the love that flows as justice" (p. 36), but "to celebrate our sexuality is to make a theological and anthropological affirmation of the pulsating dynamic of created life, the force within us that moves us beyond ourselves toward others" (p. 76). Our sexuality is nowhere more powerful or more sacred and resanctified than in our compassionate, loving, fecund efforts toward justice and liberation (cf., Clark, 1989).

As gay men and lesbians in an erotophobic and AIDS-phobic culture, we have a unique vocation regarding our sexuality and all human sexuality. If we can set aside our lingering (homo)sexual guilt and resolve the dualisms of body/spirit, sexuality/spirituality, and sex/love, we will then be able to resanctify and celebrate our sexuality in safe and responsible ways, apart from the procreatively functional and gender role reinforcing patterns given by our patriarchal enculturation. In so doing, we can also discover both a heightened awareness of the value of our sexual partners and a deepened sense of human intimacy and affection--for one another and for our whole community. We can similarly recognize and touch both the spiritual power latent in caring acts of sexual love and the fecund communal empowerment we need for the tasks of liberation (Clark, 1989). Ultimately, as we are able to genuinely and fully embrace our gay being and our gay selves as sanctified and good, as we are able to dissolve duality and to resacramentalize our sexuality, and as we are able to embody balance in our lives--intimately interdependent with a God who stands with us as compassion and empowerment for justice-seeking and liberation--through all these activities will we discover, create, nourish, and sustain our wholeness as gay people (Clark, 1989). We will learn, in fact, to live within the paradox(es), between the opposites in a creative tension begetting balance and wholeness.[4] Moreover, such a radical reclamation and reaffirmation of our vision of sexuality can enable us to move on in our pilgrimage, from theory (vision) to praxis (reality), en route to celebration. To conjoin theory and praxis, therefore, entails wrestling with the realities of our gay/lesbian relationships, examining both our current options (monogamy/nonmonogamy) and their related issues (jealousy, envy, fidelity), as well as our models for prophetic reevaluation and continuing growth as both a sexual and liberational people.

* * *

III. Monogamy, Nonmonogamy, and Other Related Issues

(i) The Dilemma of Choosing

As patriarchy progressively shaped not only western culture, but western religio-moral codes and legal structures as well, celibacy and heterosexual monogamy gradually became the only acceptable models for sexual relationships. Although as gay men and lesbians we find ourselves marginal to this entire system of heterosexist moral and legal structures (and protections), we nevertheless fall under the powerful influence of its values and models. Merely accepting our gay/lesbian identity, even at the most fundamental and all-encompassing levels, does not automatically free us from the impact of our enculturation to endorse monogamy as the only form for our most intimate relationships. That enculturation is part of the baggage we bring to our theological and ethical reflections. In her recent, reflective study of gay/lesbian couples, Berzon (1988) has astutely described the complexity of our dilemma--of the baggage we bring to this issue--as the unwitting heirs of patriarchy and heterosexism:

> Each partner brings to [a] relationship an ideological stance on the monogamy issue, which is the combined product of the pattern in their family, their moral training, their gender-role conditioning, the current standards of [their particular gay/lesbian sub-community], and their personal sexual history. Each partner also brings her/his own particular level of tolerance for uncertainty that influences how much he or she can put up with potentially threatening nonmonogamous activity by a partner. (p. 210)

Unlike our heterosexual counterparts in some significant ways, however, we are more free, as gay men and lesbians, to critically evaluate relationship patterns and to choose whether we will engage in or make commitments to monogamous or nonmonogamous relation-

ships.   We are frequently already outside the demands
of procreativity and the typical constraints of nuclear
family life, and we have also begun to realize that
even the harsh realities of AIDS within our community
need not force monogamy upon us.   We have begun to realize, for example, that "safe-sex" practices allow us
many of the same freedoms and sexual variety that we
experienced before AIDS (cf., Marcus, 1988).   Consequently, we still bear both the freedom and the burden
of choice, regarding how we will construct our sexual
relationships.   We may even find that our decisions
about monogamy vs. nonmonogamy are constantly in need
of reappraisal and fresh decision-making.

Certainly no consensus yet exists within the gay
and lesbian communities as to which is preferable,
monogamy or some idiosyncratic form of nonmonogamy.
Lee (1988), for example, describes a spectrum of gay/
lesbian opinion ranging from that of individuals who
believe nonmonogamy is immoral to that of those who
consider objections to nonmonogamy overly moralistic.
For those of us constantly (re)evaluating and making
new choices, as well as for those newly self-discovered
gays/lesbians among us, the absence of viable and pro-
ven alternative models to hetero-monogamy and this di-
vergence of opinion about monogamy vs. nonmonogamy are
further complicated by statistical studies of how ex-
isting gay/lesbian couples have structured their own
relationships.   Mendola (1980), for example, reported
that only 64% of her total sample of both gay and lesbian couples were monogamous and only 37% of her gay
male couples.   Alternatives to sexual exclusivity were
various, as summarized below:

	Total Sample (Gay Male & Lesbian Couples)	Gay Male Couples Only
sexual exclusivity	64%	37%
occasional outside sex	29%	49%
regular sex both out-side and within the primary relationship	4%	8%
sex outside only; no sex between the lovers	3%	6%

(data compilation from Mendola [1980], pp. 67-68)

In marked contrast to Mendola's (1980) composite total of 63% nonmonogamy among the partners in her gay male couples, McWhirter and Mattison (1984) subsequently reported that "for all couples in our study, some outside sexual activity had begun by the end of [the fifth year]. Often it had begun in [the second or third year]" (p. 69). In short, 100% of their long term gay male couples were nonmonogamous: "All couples with a relationship lasting more than five years have incorporated some provision for outside sexual activity in their relationships" (p. 252, cf., p. 285). McWhirter and Mattison (1984) did, however, acknowledge that their 100% nonmonogamy figure might ultimately be too high:

> We believe there is a trend toward more sexual exclusivity in the future. Currently [1983-1984] it is being propelled by [AIDS] . . . but we believe there is a more conservative undercurrent flowing, and more and more individuals are expressing the desire for sexual exclusivity. (p. 291, cf., Berzon, 1988))

More recently still, Kurdek and Schmitt (1988) disagree with both of these higher percentages for nonmonogamy among gay men and insist, consequently, that openness to outside sexual activity need not be the "inevitable outcome" of a relationship's development (p. 229); they report a more conservative 47% nonmonogamy among the partners in their gay male couples after five years (p. 225). Moreover, they also recognize the ambiguity behind their statistics: While "relationship longevity" correlates with open relationships, higher overall "relationship quality" and less tension correspond with closed relationships. Their open couples seem more traditionally masculine-identified, but also more tense and less satisfied overall--although they stay together longer--while their closed couples experience less tension, due in part from the "absence of conflict regarding sexual contacts outside of the relationship"--although they nevertheless break up sooner (p. 230). Short term monogamy is thus offset by longer term nonmonogamous relationships, virtually providing a comparable sexual variety over a given lifespan.

Clearly, the relationship of monogamy/nonmonogamy to other problems within a relationship cannot in itself be determinative for our decision-making process; neither resorting to or returning to monogamy, nor opening a closed relationship necessarily solves rela-

tional problems. Either closing or opening a relationship may only prove to be a sexual means to avoid confronting problems which should be discussed and resolved apart from the monogamy/nonmonogamy issue (Marcus, 1988, cf., Berzon, 1988)). While nonmonogamy may
throw relationship issues into relief--focusing, en-
larging, and exacerbating other problems, through all
too easy comparisons with idealized but less intimate
outside sexual partners--or allow and encourage issue
avoidance, monogamy may equally well function as a
blinder to, a clamp on, other issues. Partners must
instead face problems and nurture sensitive perception,
reasoned discussion, and compassionate resolution. Mutuality, clear communication, and shared, committed
process are the key, not monogamy or nonmonogamy alone:
"Any problem within the relationship is a mutual problem, not just 'his' problem or 'your' problem" (Marcus,
1988, p. 239, cf., Berzon, 1988).

With seemingly no alternative models to hetero-
monogamy, no consensus of opinion, no statistics which
do not appear contradictory, and no guaranteed correla-
tion between relational patterns and both longevity and
long term satisfaction, we are confronted with the
simple reality that neither monogamy nor nonmonogamy
are easy options. Neither one is "necessary" for gay
men or lesbians, even in the age of AIDS. We are, instead, thrown back upon the hard work--the freedom and
the burden--of deciding for ourselves and of acknowledging, confronting, and resolving the difficulties
those decisions entail (cf., Marcus, 1988). As DeCecco
(1988) admits, "There is no ideal [solution]; each
couple must find its own" (p. 3). The challenge thus
becomes that of again reaching shared, mutual choices
within our relationships, rather than making assumptions regarding our partner's desires, and thereafter
constantly discussing, evaluating, and accommodating
(cf., Berzon, 1988). Both Marcus (1988) and Berzon
(1988) emphasize the importance of ongoing communication about this issue and/or decision, as well as a
commitment not only to finding what will work best for
both partners, but also to nurturing and sustaining the
primary relationship over time. Moreover, agreements
must be constantly evaluated and (re)negotiated, remaining flexible enough to accommodate changing needs
and including frank discussions of what each partner
really wants and/or values, apart from any social or
political peer pressure. Uhrig (1984) expresses a similar conclusion:

It is perfectly acceptable, even in the lesbian
and gay world, to elect a monogamous relationship
and it is a healthy, responsible choice--but only
if it is the clear and unequivocal selection of
both partners in the relationship.
. . . What matters is not being "open" or
"closed" to outside sexual experiences; what
matters is that two people reach an honest and
trusting agreement about what they want and expect
from each other and that they live by that agreement. Honesty and faithfulness to the agreement
are the critical components. (pp. 56, 58, emphases
added)

He further concludes that the freedom of an open relationship should exist "only in the context of a responsible relationship that affirms the worth of each person" (p. 82); conversely, "relationships which use and
abuse the partner or oneself do not possess moral
value" (p. 112). Given the difficulties of making a
decision, the need for constant reevaluation, and the
importance of mutuality in the process, all without
easy solutions or guideposts, our best recourse, apart
from studied examination of our own past and/or present
relationships and our own personalities and values, may
be to examine both nonmonogamy and monogamy in greater
detail. While we may indeed find no panaceas, we may
find some practical tools for our decisions, for our
efforts to conjoin theory and praxis.

(ii) The Advantages and Problems of Nonmonogamy

If indeed we need not feel compelled into monogamy
by AIDS, as long as we absolutely and consistently follow safe-sex guidelines (cf., Appendix A), then nonmonogamy continues to be a viable option for us. Even
conservative writer Marcus (1988) admits that,

. . . There are couples who make nonmonogamy
work . . . by spending considerable amounts of
time talking about it, considering the type of ar-
rangement that best suits them . . . and that
gives them the best chance of achieving a loving,
sexual, long term relationship together. They do
not, however, use outside sexual involvements to
avoid problems in their relationship, or use outside sex as a substitute for sex with their
lovers. (p. 41)

For many gay men, at least, this choice of non-monogamy derives from our socialization as males; non-monogamy becomes our means for both acting out and coping with our enculturation to seek sexual variety and to downplay eroticism as intimacy increases. McWhirter and Mattison (1984), for example, emphasize the extent to which the "equality and similarities found in male couples are formidable obstacles to continuing high sexual vitality" over the course of long term relationships (p. 134). They are aware that increasing familiarity and comfortableness frequently reduce sexual interest and that gay men must find unique ways to keep healthy erotic tension alive. Outside sexual partners and other forms of distancing create the necessary resistance: "Almost intuitively, by developing greater independence [and self-esteem] and by introducing outside sexual partners, some couples reestablish a level of resistance that stimulates sexual interest and activity again" (p. 94). Because they assume, therefore, that nonmonogamy need not always threaten a primary relationship, they go on to suggest a secondary benefit of nonmonogamy as well, the ability of some gay men to relinquish enculturated possessiveness:

> We believe that the single most important factor that keeps couples together past the ten-year mark is the lack of possessiveness they feel, [whereas] ownership of each other sexually can become the greatest internal threat to their staying together. (p. 256)

Choosing nonmonogamy thus assumes sociopolitical dimensions, especially for gay men: While on the one hand it appears to entail an unreflective acting out of our heterosexist male socialization to seek sexual variety, conquest, and objectification, on the other hand a healthy, humanizing, and unthreatening nonmonogamy can enable gay men (and lesbians) to relinquish both hetero-monogamy as a relational model and the possessiveness that model has often reinforced, benefits which Lee (1988) asserts can only be healthy and liberating:

> Both gay and straight share socialization into the same "romantic" heritage that emphasizes the search for one fulfilling relationship, a possessive coupling with that person, and a residual bitterness if the relationship does not work out. Gays need liberation from this . . . view before

they can enjoy satisfying . . . relationships.
(pp. 30-31)

Nonmonogamy is no panacea, however; neither renewed sexual interest between primary partners nor an
easy relinquishing of possessiveness by the individuals
involved is ever guaranteed. Marcus (1988), for example, recognizes that vocational and life issues, as
well as AIDS-related anxiety and loss, also contribute
to waning sexual interest within couplings, and he specifically cautions gay male partners that both declin-
ing sexual interest and considerations of nonmonogamy
require frequent reassurances of love and commitment,
between the primary relationship partners, if the situation is to remain nonthreatening. In other words, despite the ideal advantages of having sexual variety and
of developing nonpossessiveness, real lived nonmonogamy
is not without its problems.
While there is no true consensus as to whether
nonmonogamy really works for couples over prolonged
periods of time (cf., Mendola, 1980), there is evidence
that the question of whether to maintain an exclusive
sexual relationship is a "universal conflict," particularly for gay male couples. Comments Silverstein
(1981), for example, "Outside sex . . . is by far the
most common source of conflict in every gay male relationship" (p. 130, cf., pp. 140-141). And whether the
percentage of gay male nonmonogamy is really 47% (Kurdek and Schmitt, 1988), 63% (Mendola, 1980), 100%
(McWhirter and Mattison, 1984), or some other figure,
Silverstein (1981) concludes that "very few" individuals actually manage real long term monogamy (p. 339):
"It is a rare couple that has stayed together for any
length of time without [at least some] sex outside the
relationship" (p. 184). Consequently, the first problem with nonmonogamy is that it is always at least a
potential source, if not an actual source, of conflict.
As gay men, few of us appear to have completely set
aside our hetero-monogamous (possessive and competitive) enculturation, although McWhirter and Mattison
(1984) are willing to argue that nonmonogamy presents
less of a problem (less conflict) after a couple has
been together nearly a decade!
Mendola (1980) takes the potential for conflict
present in nonmonogamy one step further, rightfully insisting that while sex is not the main ingredient in
any long term committed relationship, it is still an
important and necessary element. Consequently, a partner's constant outside sexual activity, particularly a

need or even drivenness to find sex outside the primary
relationship on a regular or routine basis, does not
seem functional either to a relationship's healthy en-
durance or to both partners having the necessary energy
to focus upon one another or upon relational maintenance and growth. In her own more recent study, Berzon
(1988) has also elaborated on the extent to which an
unreflective shift into nonmonogamy, particularly a
compulsive nonmonogamy, can become threatening to one
or both primary partners:

> People in officially monogamous relationships
> sometimes use outside sexual experiences to ex-
> press dissatisfaction with something in the [pri-
> mary] partnership. Sometimes it is . . . bold and
> blatant. . . . Sometimes it is more subtle, the
> partner[s] not quite sure what is happening but
> knowing that something is wrong.
>   . . . People who look outside their relation-
> ship for relief of [vague or unarticulated] part-
> nership tension do not [appear to] trust their
> partner's ability to understand, to care, or to
> change. (pp. 211-212)

A drastic change or an irreversible decrease in
sexual activity between primary partners works against
a relationship; constant outside sex may lead not to
the ideal of renewed eroticism between primary partners
(cf., McWhirter and Mattison, 1984), but toward a decreasing sensitivity to needs and nurturance within the
primary relationship, thereby exacerbating other problems (Mendola, 1980). Importantly, this dilemma may
arise not so much from possessiveness about outside
sexual acts as from the loss of any emotional and psychological intimacy which outside sex unwittingly deflects from the primary relationship (cf., Mendola,
1980). Ultimately, outside sexual activity may seriously affect the level of intimacy, as well as sexual
interest, within the primary relationship, resulting in
a vague sense of insecurity and/or fear for either or
both partners. Silverstein (1981), for example, concludes that sexual activity and emotional intimacy
within a relationship can become stale as a result of
the fear of potential changes in either partner or in
the relationship itself, as a result of the fear of the
direction(s) in which these changes might lead either
partner or the relationship, and as a result of avoiding "the potential intimacy of working together toward
a readjusted relationship" (p. 179). In any case,

Berzon (1988) cautions primary partners to examine and resolve their real relationship issues apart from either their choices or their other issues regarding outside sexual activity.

Nonmonogamy's third problem, exacerbating both conflict within and insecurities about the primary relationship, emerges whenever one or the other partner forms a friendship which includes sex and excludes, and thereby threatens, the unincluded partner (McWhirter and Mattison, 1984). Outside emotional involvement with sexual friendships clearly deflects intimacy from the primary relationship (Silverstein, 1981), although McWhirter and Mattison (1984) insist that even this state of affairs does not have to be fatal for the primary relationship:

> The development of a new limerence by one or both partners . . . does become somewhat disconcerting to partners . . . when they do not realize the usual transient nature of the feelings and experience the terrifying threat of relationship dissolution. . . . Couples . . . must allow each other the freedom to have such new romances but must also safeguard their mateship with mutual agreements and understandings about the new [outside partners]. (p. 95)

What the naive idealism of McWhirter's and Mattison's (1984) view overlooks is that the "terrifying threat of relationship dissolution" may be overwhelming, undermining either or both partner's confidence in and hope for the primary relationship's survival. When that hope is lost, the energy and willingness to resolve other relationship issues and problems may also evaporate, plunging the relationship not toward only an imagined and feared end, but toward a real point of termination (Mendola, 1980).[5]

Most recently, Marcus (1988) has handily summarized the various problems which we must confront when we choose nonmonogamous relationships. Not surprisingly, his discussion simply confirms the findings of the earlier studies. Recognizing that with gay male relationships the initial passion "almost universally" does not last (p. 135), he nevertheless describes the variety of problems facing nonmonogamous couples: (1) increasing emotional anxiety and instability (vague insecurities and fears); (2) intensifying relationship difficulties and too much distancing (intimacy issues); and, (3) decreasing sexual interest between partners

and increasing problems when outside sex becomes emotionally involving (relationship threat). Finally, regarding this third and most difficult problem to sur-
mount, if nonmonogamy is ever to be workable, Silverstein (1981) admits that "differences between lovers
over outside affairs are the primary reason for the
breakup of [gay male] love relationship[s]" (p. 339).
That fact alone might lead us to disavow nonmonogamy as
a genuine option. Silverstein (1981), however, immediately adds that "these conflicts often reflect other
problems in a relationship, such as jealousy, envy, dependence, and intimacy" (p. 339). Again and again are
we reminded that while nonmonogamy is a problem-filled,
non-panaceac option, resorting to a hetero-monogamous
model often simplistically avoids other issues, issues
which must also be examined before an authentic choice
between monogamy and nonmonogamy is possible.

(iii) The Demons of Jealousy, Envy, and Low Self-Esteem

Whether we ultimately choose monogamy or nonmonogamy as our particular framework for constructing our
relationships, we owe it to ourselves to be sure that
we are making our decision(s) for the right reasons,
that we are not avoiding deeper issues with those decisions. Importantly, the overlapping human emotions of
jealousy and envy frequently complicate and confuse our
decision-making processes. Moreover, only by enhancing
our abilities both to distinguish between these two
emotions and to resolve their independent and specific
conflicts, can we then work to strengthen and deepen
our relationships (Berzon, 1988). Despite commonly
held beliefs to the contrary, Lee (1988), for example,
insists that jealousy is really related to our personal
insecurities and not to our love for another person.
Similarly, Silverstein (1981) distinquishes between
jealousy, as "enmity motivated by . . . the fear of
abandonment," and envy, as enmity "motivated by competitiveness or covetousness . . ., resentful of another
person's perceived superiority or success"; envy develops whenever there is a perceived "competition between
lovers in which one partner sees himself [sic.] as second best" (p. 150). For gay men in particular, whenever we open our relationships to outside sexual experiences, our fears that our partners may find someone
else whom they prefer romantically and sexually (jealousy) becomes confused by our enculturated urge to make
comparisons (envy). Victims of the male socialization
process, we unwittingly compare our sexual capabilities

-44-

and performances with those of the outsiders who attract our lovers and, more damagingly, we compare the
numbers--how many new men "he" attracts vs. how many
"I" attract.   What may have begun as a harmless nonmonogamy can spiral into a relationship threatening
competition.
    Our confused jealousy/envy also gets further com-
plicated whenever we come face to face with a common
gay male double-standard: We know ourselves well
enough to know what our true loyalties are; we know we
will return to our partners, still fully loving and
committed to them, but we fear that our partners' loyalties are not as clear, that they may not return (cf.,
McWhirter and Mattison, 1984).   Fear and distrust, not
nonmonogamy as such, are the real culprits, as McWhirter and Mattison (1984) elaborate:

        The biggest difficulty we uncovered in the
    discussion on this issue was the intellectual and
    emotional dichotomy the couples experience in put-
    ting [nonmonogamy] into practice.   In principle
    most accept the idea of sex play with others, but
    when their partner exercises the option, feelings
    of jealousy, fear of loss and abandonment, or just
    plain anger frequently erupt. . . . Many men say
    they recognize their double standard.   "It's OK
    for me to have sex with someone else because I
    know how I feel about you, but it's not OK for you
    to do the same thing."   The undelivered communica-
    tion in these cases is, "because I can't or don't
    really trust you."   It is a heritage of male
    training in our culture. (p. 255)

As long as gay men allow ourselves unreflectively to be
shaped by our enculturation as males to compete with,
rather than to love and nurture, one another, we will
transcend neither our distrustful double standard nor
the confusion of jealousy/envy, all of which are still
further complicated by issues of self-esteem.
    For gay men in particular, enculturated in both a
heterosexist and homophobic society, our self-esteem is
always difficult to sustain and requires constant nurturance against unwittingly internalized negative
stereotypes (Fortunato, 1983, Laner, 1988, cf., Clark,
1989).   The impact of homophobia, lowering our self-esteem and undercutting our self-worth, is frequently
manifest as sexual inhibition or shame, insecurity,
jealousy, and envy (Berzon, 1988, Lee, 1988).   McNeill
(1988) even goes so far as to insist that "one cannot

build a healthy, lasting relationship if one still har-
bors feelings of self-hatred and shame," or of unresolved, internalized homophobia (p. 71). Conversely,
Lee (1988) has also observed that,

> . . . Gay males who have fully internalized
> the gay consciousness and are truly "proud to be
> gay" are less likely to suffer the lack of self-
> esteem. . . . There is clearly an ideological re-
> lationship between gay liberation and a less jeal-
> ous, more playful love style. (p. 28)

Similarly, Mendola (1980) and Uhrig (1984) also argue
that a healthy gayself-acceptance and self-love--genu-
ine gayself-esteem--are necessary for a healthy and
whole relationship. We must believe in our own personal value, in the validity and integrity of our personal value system(s), and in the absolute value of our
relationships. While compromising ourselves--doubting
our personal values or questioning our self-worth as
gay/lesbian people--can only hurt our relationships
(Mendola, 1980), full gayself-acceptance or "gay liberation consciousness" can enable a deeper, "more honest
intimacy" (Lee, 1988, p. 28). Uhrig (1984) even goes
so far as to insist that self-esteem/self-acceptance is
ultimately more important to a successful relationship
than physical attraction or sexual capabilities.
And, of course, when our self-esteem is low, whenever we are especially vulnerable to homophobic and
other negative messages, we are also more susceptible
to feelings of jealousy and envy. Within a competitive, gay male open relationship, a sense that one
partner is "losing the competition" exacerbates low
self-esteem and a vicious circle ensues. Silverstein
(1981) insightfully elaborates:

> This competition is not a pleasant business, since
> it is inevitably mixed with feelings of love and
> compassion for one's lover. Yet still another in-
> gredient is added, feelings of [low] self-esteem.
> . . . One member of the pair does not feel as com-
> petent sexually as the other. . . . The key is
> that he believes, rightly or wrongly, that in a
> head-on competition with his lover . . . he would
> surely lose. . . . Behind [his] tears is the wish
> that he could be as good at attracting other men
> or felt the freedom to roam sexually that his
> lover does.

> By and large, men sexually envious of their
> lover's ability to attract other men want to do
> exactly the same thing. Instead of developing
> their own abilities, they interfere with the
> lover's capabilities. In this way, the envious
> man remains forever convinced of his own incompe-
> tence, and it is this reinforcement of feelings of
> low self-worth that does the most damage. . . .
> While all sorts of methods may be chosen to ex-
> press envy, very few will help the relationship,
> which is presumably what both lovers want. (pp.
> 185, 156)

The cycle of competition, low self-esteem, envy, and
jealousy/fear of abandonment necessarily affects relational intimacy and, if unbroken, may propel partners
into more and more outside sex and competition. Just
as "intimacy is always threatening to the person who
lacks self-affirmation" (Nelson, 1978, pp. 116-117),
so, as jealousy/envy intensify and partners spend less
time together, they risk creating too much distance between themselves, further undermining intimacy (McWhirter and Mattison, 1984). Accumulating jealousy/envy,
falling self-esteem, and dissipating intimacy can fuel
the confusion and grief which undercut relational maintenance and plunge a relationship and its partners into
despair and breaking up.

Fortunately, the demons of jealousy, envy, and low
self-esteem are not invincible. We begin to assault
them offensively whenever we can reaffirm our gayself-
worth. Coming-out, revaluing our gay/lesbian being and
sexuality, and healing the wounds of homophobia and
heterosexist enculturation start us on our way (Fortunato, 1983, Clark, 1989). Refusing to be victims and
defiantly celebrating who we are, both privately and
sociopolitically, begins to raise our self-esteem,
freeing us from a certain unnecessary (and unhealthy)
dependence upon our partners and enabling us to confront our jealousy, fear, and envy:

> Intimacy rests in some large measure upon each
> partner's own sense of worth as a person, each
> one's ability to be self-affirming. Without this,
> we elevate the other into the center of our lives,
> hoping that the other's affirmation will assure us
> of our own reality. But this is too large an or-
> der for the partner. (Nelson, 1978, p. 116)

Just as we may become unwittingly ensnared in a vicious cycle of jealousy, envy, competition, and self-denigration, so we may also consciously construct a nexus which heals us individually and which renews our relationships.

First of all, we can refuse to belittle or undervalue either our own feelings or those of our partners. We can, in fact, simultaneously nurture one another's value (self-worth) and take seriously one another's feelings, without assuming responsibility for those feelings. Marcus (1988), for example, speaks specifically to gay men when he says, "If your lover tends to be jealous of the attention [other] men give you, you may be able to help him feel less threatened, but you can't _force_ him not to feel jealous" (p. 25, emphasis added). Berzon (1988) also encourages us to respect and to listen to our feelings, particularly those of jealously and envy: "Uncharacteristic" or "unusual" jealousy can serve as an "early warning signal that something in the relationship needs more attention" and that we should address those issues (p. 162). Jealousy cannot be simplistically overlooked as only a negative and/or undesirable emotion between primary partners:

> Jealousy . . . should be heeded as a warning that something in the person, or in the relationship, needs attention.
> Paying attention to a partner's jealous feelings, rather than dismissing [trivializing or resenting] them, can deepen understanding of that person's emotional needs [thus also deepening relational intimacy]. (p. 164)

In addition both to attending to the importance of our feelings and to committing ourselves to resolving their underlying issues together, we can also consciously act and speak, particularly within our non-monogamous primary relationships, so as to reassure our partners of our real loyalties and of their value to us personally, erotically, and sexually. We can actively refuse to take our partner's trust and commitment for granted, and we can choose to moderate and/or even temporarily forego outside sexual activity for a time, in order to ease our partners' anxieties (cf., McWhirter and Mattison, 1984). At the same time we can also refuse to create emotionally dependent situations and, instead, help each other to stand gay-proudly and assertively interdependent within our healing and renew-

ing relationships.   Silverstein (1981) insightfully
elaborates:

> There are no quick cures for jealousy and
> envy. Most men who feel deeply wounded want the
> pain to go away, but the only way to accomplish
> this is to experience greater pain and trust again
> in the person who holds the power to hurt--one's
> own lover. Only when discussion between lovers is
> honest, when each can understand the perspective
> of the other, can there be any real resolution of
> the conflict. . . . If the lovers can [avoid mu-
> tual accusations and] express their feelings about
> the situation and their feelings of vulnerability
> without demanding anything of the other, then the
> probability of resolution increases. To achieve
> it, both [partners] need to be willing to change,
> be ready to relinquish their roles of victimizer
> and victim, and accept responsibility for their
> actions. (p. 157)

Once again, compassionate negotiation and a willingness
to risk more vulnerability can lead to healing and
deeper, stronger intimacy. Confronting our issues and
our hurting, while eschewing the victim role, can lead
us to a healthy, reaffirming interdependence. Battling
the demons of jealousy, envy, and low self-esteem can
open us and our partners together to a heightened capacity for risk-taking and growth (cf., Berzon, 1988).
   McWhirter and Mattison (1984) argue that taking
risks with/in our gay male relationships, redeveloping
autonomy and independence, as well as learning to balance dependence/independence, separation/return, participation at home/in the world, are all necessary for
the growth and deepening of our relationships. Nonmonogamy, as one example, enables partners to take
risks, to test the soundness of the relationship itself
and to evaluate levels of trust and self-esteem, as
well as to circumvent potential boredom and to recreate
optimal erotic distance. When the partners always come
home to, and reaffirm the value of, the primary relationship and of each other, these actions can help to
assuage the fears which feed jealousy and envy. With
steady, empathetic reassurances, two men can ideally
test and rebalance the dynamics of their relationship
and develop an ever more realistic clarity about their
own and their partner's expectations and capacities for
meeting needs. As McWhirter and Mattison (1984) com-
ment, "Men learn that they can move away from the rela-

tionship and gain confidence that each will be present and available to the other upon return" (p. 64).

Of course, risk-taking and rediscovered autonomy in balance with a relationship clearly does not require outside sexual encounters; outside sex is only one form of risk-taking. While nonmonogamous couples may be able to withstand the battles over jealousy, envy, and low self-esteem, and ultimately grow stronger and more intimate as a result, nonmonogamy is not our only option (cf., Kurdek and Schmitt, 1988). Moreover, numerous gay liberationist writers insist that a mutual and well-informed decision for monogamy, a decision which does not avoid these more difficult issues but which wrestles with them authentically en route to decision, can be a legitimate gay-affirmative option for us (cf., DeCecco, 1988, Marcus, 1988, Uhrig, 1984). We may even be able to construct monogamous relationships which do not merely imitate heterosexist models, and for this reason alone, we must examine monogamy as well before we make our own decisions.

(iv) The Rationale and Values behind Monogamy

While McWhirter and Mattison (1984) refreshingly and joyfully imply that our gay male (and lesbian) sexuality may include "recreational" (nonmonogamous) aspects and still retain a special, even sacramental quality within a couple's life together, Edwards (1984) more cautiously suggests that authentic, sacramental love needs time to develop, to deepen, and to become genuinely self-giving and mutually nurturant. Counseling constancy (monogamy) rather than promiscuity or sexual variety (nonmonogamy), he insists that "liberating love" or "commitment in love" requires both "steadfast caring" and a capacity for "suffering through," qualities of a deepened love relationship between two people which can only develop over time (pp. 118, 119). Even the liberal pre-AIDS scholar of gay male couples, Silverstein (1981), clearly elucidates a variety of perfectly good reasons by which we might prefer monogamy. He realizes, for example, the influence of our enculturation, that monogamy remains a powerful romantic ideal imbued with religio-moral, personal, and even aesthetic value for many gay/lesbian people. He respectfully acknowledges the very real strength of our fears of loss, abandonment, and aloneness/loneliness; our fears that one outside sexual encounter only leads to another and another such encounter, until a primary relationship is undermined; and, our experiences of

homophobia and its resultant low self-esteem. Finally,
he acknowledges the purely pragmatic value of gay/les-
bian monogamy, realizing that "the energy required to
find third parties and to coordinate them with the
[primary] relationship" always diverts energy from the
intimacy required to sustain and nourish the primary
relationship (p. 145). In short, monogamy may simply--
and quite legitimately--feel more "right" for us in the
depths of our being.

Ironically, perhaps, the one writer whose work not
only bears an empathetic kinship with the concerns of
Edwards (1984) and Silverstein (1981), but which goes
on to discuss monogamy at length, is non-gay theologian
Nelson (1978). While we may not always agree with him,
the fact that he is so strongly supportive of gay men
and lesbians and of our sexuality and our relationships
(cf., Nelson, 1977) requires that we at least hear him
out and dialogue with him as part of our gay/lesbian
theological and ethical reflections on this issue.
While Nelson (1978) recognizes that a committed relationship "without libido and romantic attraction is
less than full," he does not advise outside sexual experiences to re-eroticize a primary relationship, because "sexual and romantic attraction without genuine
friendship is also an invitation to disappointment and
distortion" (p. 113). He is equally aware of the extent to which outside, sexual "genuine friendships" can
threaten a primary relationship. Recognizing the reality of human jealousy and the pain of our insecurities,
he is convinced that multiple or divided sexual interests diminish not only our gratification and our fulfillment (nurturing a sense that we never get enough of
whatever it is we need), but our primary intimacy as
well. In short, however compassionately we might in-
tend it, nonmonogamy always risks hurting the single
most important other person in our lives--our partners:

> Even . . . in an open [relationship] where there
> is no deception, the [partner] left out of [the
> outside] relationship is bound to feel rejection.
> One of the sexual relationships is bound to be ne-
> glected, and it will probably be the [primary re-
> lationship]. (p. 145)

To diffuse jealousy and fear of loss, Nelson (1978)
counsels developing genital exclusivity but without
possessive ownership, attempting to encourage simultaneously both nonpossessive monogamy and individual
autonomy.

Nelson's (1978) other major concern is that outside sex most frequently becomes objectifying and dehumanizing. If outside sex is purely for physical gratification, treating the body as an instrument or as a
pleasure-machine, the patriarchal and alienating body/
spirit and sex/love dualisms reemerge, trivializing
both the individuals involved and our sexuality itself;
he is deeply concerned whenever our sexual behavior
trivializes either ourselves or other persons:

> If I desire another sexually without wanting to
> have deep knowledge of the other, without wanting
> to be in living communion with the partner, I am
> treating the other merely as object, as instru-
> ment, as means to my self-centered gratification.
> (p. 32)

Importantly, just because two gay men, for example,
agree to treat each other as sexual objects for a few
hours, mutually aware and fully accepting of those
terms, that alone does not necessarily circumvent the
trivialization which can occur. Asserting that caring,
commitment, profound respect, and "openness to life"
together constitute genuinely responsible human sexuality, he consequently insists that if the exception to
monogamy (any outside sexual encounter) is admitted,
then "the burden of proof must be borne--that this
[outside] sexual sharing realistically promises to enhance and not damage the capacity for interpersonal fidelity and personal wholeness" in all of the affected
relationships (p. 151). Moreover, he argues, "There
appears to be a direct connection between emotional maturity, on the one hand, and the wedding of sexual expression to love, tenderness, and relational depth, on
the other" (p. 157).
    For those of us trying to evaluate and to decide
how we want to construct our own gay/lesbian relationships, particularly for those of us whose patterns already tend toward some degree of nonmonogamy, Nelson's
(1978) prophetic challenge is a difficult one to hear.
Neither nonmonogamous coupling, nor uncoupled sexual
variety, is in any sense morally wrong a priori; no
prohibition of these options is carved in stone by a
divine or any other authority. These options do, however, require a great deal of energy and compassionate
sensitivity in order to ensure fairness--justice--to
all involved persons, as well as to ensure that no affected relationship or individual is ever devalued or
dehumanized. In other words, not only are we con-

fronted with the difficulty of maintaining the special, even sacramental, aspects of our primary sexual and emotional relationship(s) in balance with our outside sexual encounters (cf., McWhirter and Mattison, 1984); now we must also ponder how not to make those encounters alienating and objectifying, on the one hand, and how not to exclude our partners or threaten our primary relationships if those encounters do develop humanizing sexual friendships, on the other hand. If all our sexual relationships embody a similar level of humanizing compassion (love), how can our primary partners, or how can we, not feel threatened?

Clearly, choosing between monogamy and nonmonogamy for a pattern or model for our relationships is not an easy task. Monogamy avoids many of the problems of nonmonogamy, from the tension caused by jealousy/envy to the trivialization/objectification of our sexuality, and it embodies some very admirable values. The reality among gay men in particular, though, is that strictly monogamous relationships, however satisfying, are often short-lived (cf., Kurdek and Schmitt, 1988). Nonmonogamy, by contrast, is at least as difficult if not more difficult to practice successfully. Attempting to sustain a long term nonmonogamous primary relationship requires that we always be willing to deal with tension, to work on our feelings of jealousy and envy, and to sort out those issues from issues of self-esteem. It requires constantly battling homophobic messages from our culture, which threaten our self-acceptance and our self-esteem, and living utterly vulnerable before, and trusting of, the loyalty and compassion of our partners and of the soundness of our relationships. Finally, it means seeking that ideal balance which transcends both a patriarchal possessiveness of our primary partners and a patriarchal objectification/trivialization/dehumanization of our outside partners, while simultaneously not allowing our outside sexual friendships to become a threat to our primary sexual friend and lover.

Whether, or to what extent, such an ideal balancing act is possible, for the wholeness of all concerned parties, clearly remains an open question. Certainly, for those of us wishing to at least consider this difficult option, some consideration must also be given to what guidelines we will use to shape our nonmonogamous gay/lesbian sexuality-in-relationship. Moreover, nonmonogamy in the context of long term committed, and somehow sacramental, relationships also challenges us to rethink the meaning of fidelity as a concept broader

than mere genital exclusivity.   If we are genuinely
freed of the hetero-monogamous model, we bear the burden and the responsibility both for constructing our
relationships and our sexual behavior, as well as for
determining exactly how we can be and will be genuinely
faithful lovers.

*   *   *

IV. Limits, Guidelines, and Genuine Fidelity

(i) Exploring Limits and Guidelines

While a traditional understanding of monogamy automatically entails specific limitations, most obviously genital exclusivity between partners, nonmonogamy carries no such automatic guidelines. Consequently, those lesbians and gay men who wish to construct open relationships, as well as those among us who are single, must consider a plethora of options. In our sexual freedom, we alone ultimately bear the burden for deciding <u>how</u> we can be responsibly and compassionately nonmonogamous. Moreover, as with our capacity to construct a healthy, whole sexuality in general, our specific capacity to develop caring self-limitation--to eschew an "anything goes" sexual ethics--also depends upon our level of genuine gayself-acceptance. While Nelson (1978), for example, argues that sexual guidelines and principles "should nurture our growth into greater maturity and responsible freedom, and not inhibit it" (p. 129), he is also convinced that our ability to so construct our sexual behavior depends upon a healthy self-love and self-acceptance. Healthy self-esteem and responsible self-limitation go hand in hand:

> Self-acceptance is related to the ability to say No. Those . . . who feel driven to accede to all requests and demands of others are expressing a consuming anxiety about their basic acceptability. The ability to say No . . . is the ability to resist the forces of depersonalization. . . . It is essential to our humanity and our being-for-others.
>   Self-acceptance thus carries with it the ability to distinguish between feelings and desires, on the one hand, and genuine needs on the other. . . . We also know that some of our desires do not represent humanly fulfilling needs. Thus we can distinguish between those which can be fulfilled with constructive and enriching effects for our-

selves and others, and those which if acted upon
might impoverish and destroy. (p. 82)

To help us avoid impoverishing our sexual interactions,
he goes on to counsel us that all our sexual acts
should be loving and life-giving, fecund in the broadest possible sense.

Given his belief that, ultimately, our sexuality
should be more informed by loving, life-giving values
than restricted by a priori rules, Nelson's (1978)
overriding concern in doing sexual ethics focuses not
upon specific sexual acts, but upon the social and interpersonal ramifications of our sexual behavior:

The willingness to assume responsibility [for] ongoing relationship and its particular commitments
. . . involves responsiveness to the partner's
continuing needs for sustaining, healing, growth--
and to one's own needs for the same. . . . Accountability also means the weighing of [actions]
in terms of [their] probable effects for the wider
community [i.e., their effects on other persons].
(p. 128)

Consequently, the guidelines which he offers for our
gay/lesbian theological and ethical reflections are
frequently reiterated by gay liberationist writers
themselves. Much like Heyward (1984), for example,
Nelson (1978) insists that sexual love must "always be
expressed as justice" (p. 126), so that it empowers all
involved persons and so that everyone involved "has
rightful access to the means for human fulfillment" (p.
127). Similarly anticipating Edwards' (1984) high valuation of "steadfast caring" in our sexuality, Nelson
(1978) further insists that "the physical expression of
one's sexuality with another person ought to be appropriate to the level of loving commitment present in
that relationship" (p. 127). Despite the message of
our patriarchal socialization, deeper commitment and
more fulfilling sexuality should go hand in hand; intimacy need not undermine eroticism! He goes on to con-
clude, therefore, that every genital act, as such,
"should be motivated by love," in a balance with our
other motives such as desire and pleasure, and that
every genital act should also "aim at human fulfillment
and wholeness" (p. 127).

Rather than endorsing moral absolutes, Nelson
(1978) thus attempts to construct sexual guidelines
which focus upon our responsibilities toward our own

and toward our partners' wholeness. Conversely, he adds, "We can surely say that acts which by their nature are loveless--coercive, debasing . . ., utterly impersonal, obsessed solely by physical gratification--such acts of whatever sexual sort are excluded" (p. 128). The ethical question becomes not is this act "right" or "wrong," but rather, does our sexual interaction both love, respect, and empower one another? Heyward (1984) synthesizes Nelson's (1978) concern for justice and fairness in our sexuality with Edwards' (1984) insistence upon steadfast caring, in her own construction of sexual love: "My passion is my willingness to suffer for us, not masochistically, but rather bearing up who we are, enduring both the pain and the pleasure of what it means to love, to do what is just, to make right our relation" (p. 87, emphasis added).

Much like Nelson (1978), Uhrig (1984) also recognizes the variety of moral perspectives which we bring to our gay/lesbian theological and ethical reflections and he consequently warns against moralism--against making either prescriptions or proscriptions--as we explore and/or develop sexual guidelines. Instead, he extends the process of raising questions for us, by breaking down the question "Is this sexual behavior both just and mutually empowering?" into a number of component questions: Does this particular sexual relationship or encounter fulfill both our needs and both our self-worth? Does it enable or restrict both our lives? Is it joyful and health-enhancing, both physically and psycho-spiritually? Is it mutual; are both partners equally concerned for the wholeness of the other? Do the various components of this relationship or encounter, including the sexual activity(ies), "enhance the dignity of each person" (p. 112, cf., pp. 111-113)? Gay liberationist writers Goodman, et al. (1983), also seek to avoid judgmentalism in their own suggestions for our reflective process. They believe that ethically sound sexual behavior should both allow for and encourage emotional depth and explore whole-body sensuality. Like Nelson (1978), their understanding of our sexuality is multi-dimensional (whole-body/ -emotions/-spirit/-genitalia) and rejects treating our bodies as alienated objects. They go on to advise us to examine all our sexual sharing, therefore, in the "context of personal growth toward autonomy and self-actualization" for all the involved persons in any sexual exchange (Goodman, et al., 1983, p. 122). Importantly, Goodman, et al. (1983), also counsel us against using sex to avoid or to disguise our other needs for affection, touching, and/or personal reassurance. They urge us to recognize our nonsexual motivations and needs and to resolve those issues appropriately, so that those needs do not distort our sexual interactions.

McWhirter and Mattison (1984) have attempted to make the abstract process of exploring and developing nonjudgmental sexual guidelines more specific, more concrete and helpful for actual, nonmonogamous gay (male) relationships. They recognize that nonmonogamy is always a somewhat threatening and unresolved situation for their couples (cf., Silverstein, 1981) and that, consequently, rules and guidelines, however specific, are always "attempts at control in an area that continues to be an elusive source of anxiety and fear for most couples" (McWhirter and Mattison, 1984, p. 259). Avoiding some of the thornier issues raised by Nelson (1978) and discussed above (Chapter 3 [iv]), they specifically recommend permitting outside sex or nonmonogamy "with clearly outlined rules about the recreational nature of that sex and a mutual promise to avoid emotional entanglements with [outside] sex partners" (McWhirter and Mattison, 1984, p. 258). The specifics of such rules, however, must be worked out idiosyncratically by each couple, although more clearly articulated and even jointly written rules, rather than vague assumptions, can ultimately reduce the tensions which nonmonogamy can cause (cf., Appendix B). More recently, Berzon (1988) has reiterated the importance of purposefully developing rules for nonmonogamy which are not only idiosyncratically appropriate to the particular needs of any two individual partners in a specific primary relationship, but which are also flexible and periodically renegotiable, in order always to accommodate the changing needs and concerns of both the individual partners and the relationship itself:

> Partnership agreements regarding [nonmonogamy] should not just evolve. They should be carefully talked through so that the [resultant] agreement reflects what each person truly wants to happen.
> [Such agreements] should be reviewed at regular intervals so they can be updated, if necessary, in accordance with the changing needs of one or both partners. (p. 164)

While any given couple may therefore work out its own flexible set of specific rules for putting nonmonogamy into practice, our gay/lesbian theological and ethical reflections and our efforts to explore guidelines are not so specific. At best a number of values begin to emerge: self-acceptance and self-limitation, responsibility for our partners and ourselves (including but certainly not limited to safe sex practices), justice/compassion/steadfast caring, and mutuality and wholism. How these values ultimately shape our real, lived sexual behavior, within monogamous or nonmonogamous couplings, or, as uncoupled and sexually active gay/lesbian individuals, may also depend upon how we understand fidelity, upon the ways in which we conceptualize how we will be genuinely faithful lovers.

(ii) Reconceptualizing Fidelity

While our patriarchal western culture has traditionally insisted that fidelity primarily means sexual exclusivity (and that, consequently, possessive jealousy is an appropriate response to "infidelity"), numerous scholarly observers of gay/lesbian couples have realized that fidelity is a much larger issue. The overall quality of a relationship and the level of emotional commitment therein are far more important than narrow, genital definitions of fidelity (cf., Marcus, 1988, McWhirter and Mattison, 1984, Mendola, 1980). McWhirter and Mattison (1984) elaborate:

> [Among our couples] fidelity is not defined in terms of sexual behavior but rather by . . . emotional commitment. . . .
> Only through time [does] the symbolic nature of sexual exclusivity translate into the real issues of faithfulness. When that happens, the substantive, emotional dependability of the partner, not sex, becomes the real measure of faithfulness.
> . . . Gay men expect mutual emotional dependability with their partners and that relationship fidelity transcends concerns about sexuality and exclusivity. (pp. 252, 285)

Reliance upon one another for mutual emotional support and friendship, as well as faithfulness to the commitment, to the relationship and to whatever agreements it entails (cf., Uhrig, 1984), are far more important than sexual issues alone, or, as Mendola (1980) comments,

"Sex is important in a committed relationship, but it is not the most important thing" (p. 63).

Commitment to the relationship, or relational fidelity, obviously includes a number of components: Communication between partners, for example, must be optimally open and mutual, including a willingness on the part of both partners to share responsibility(ies), to compromise as needed, and to work together toward a common future (Berzon, 1988, Marcus, 1988, Mendola, 1980). It entails "understanding each other, caring about each other, doing for each other," and balancing needs fulfillment both for oneself and for one's partner (Mendola, 1980, p. 63, cf., p. 65). While such commitment does not create instant security and trust, because these require time to build, commitment to the process of developing communication skills, intimacy, and growth both individually and as a couple is required as the necessary groundwork for long term compatibility (cf., Berzon, 1988, Marcus, 1988, Mendola, 1980). As partners eschew mind-reading for explicit communication and cooperation about their needs over time--from those concerning daily tasks to those concerning physical affection and even sex--a firmly grounded sense of security and trust in one another and in the relationship itself can develop (Berzon, 1988, Marcus, 1988). Ultimately, time already invested together becomes the best guarantor of a relationship's ongoing longevity.

Recently, Berzon (1988) has specifically addressed the extent to which enhanced communication skills and deepened intimacy, genital sexuality, and nongenital physical affection, are all interrelated components of genuine fidelity in our various gay/lesbian relationships. She encourages gay men and lesbians, for example, to gain more access to their emotional life and to verbalize their feelings to their partners, rather than destructively acting out buried emotions. She also specifically encourages gay/lesbian partners to discuss their sexual needs, desires, and fantasies, and thereby, to purposefully explore, experiment, and decide on sexual activities together, rather than passively allowing eroticism to wane as intimacy increases. Thoroughly convinced that deepening intimacy can enhance, rather than undermine, eroticism, she insists that "communication about sex has the potential of opening up new areas of eroticism to be explored and of integrating sexuality [and intimacy] more effectively into . . . life together" (p. 201); moreover, "being able to ask for what you want or what you no longer want is an act of faith in the relationship" (p. 208).

Also implicit in Berzon's (1988) reflections is the possibility that the _fear_ of increased intimacy between two masculinely socialized gay men, and _not_ intimacy _per se_, may actually be what threatens to de-eroticize some long term gay male relationships, as intimacy nevertheless--however slowly and painfully--develops. She consequently advises gay men, in particular, that "one can learn to look for signs that point to intimacy fears if sexual desire seems to wane in connection with developments in a relationship that symbolize growing commitment" (p. 224). Similarly, she further insists that both gay men and lesbians need to reintegrate genital sexuality and physical affection--to dissolve or reconcile the sex/love dichotomy. Not only must gay/lesbian partners (re)learn to ask for nongenital physical affection, as well as for sex; we must also remember to include some tender, supportive affection integrated within even the most passionate (or even "rough") sex: "Couples fall into a trap when the only touching they do is genital and leads to orgasm" (p. 244). Thus are our efforts to discern an ethically sound gay/lesbian sexuality again reminded not only that our capacities both for love and affection and for sexual gratification are one, but also that deepening intimacy and enhanced eroticism are _not_ necessarily mutually exclusive. Moreover, whenever we passively forfeit such integrated wholeness, therein do we allow ourselves to devalue the gift of our sexuality and the very possibilities of genuine fidelity.

Summarily, then, Nelson (1978) has outlined some practical components for genuine fidelity which are consistent with those espoused by the couples in both Mendola's (1980), Marcus' (1988), and Berzon's (1988) surveys. Fidelity, for Nelson (1978), includes commitments to both "emotional and physical intimacy" between partners, to the "growth and fulfillment of each as a person," and "to the growth of the . . . relationship itself" (p. 148). Fidelity requires "honesty, openness, and trust," as well as "a willingness to explore ways of opening the self to the partner at the deepest possible level" (p. 148). Nelson (1978) even goes so far as to concede that genuine fidelity even "includes openness to secondary relationships of emotional intimacy and potential genital expression, but with commitment to the" primary relationship (p. 148). Similarly, DeCecco (1988) has articulately summarized the pragmatic meaning of fidelity, as a broader concept than mere sexual exclusivity, as it specifically applies to actual gay male relationships:

> The gay relationship . . . represents a <u>moral</u> commitment of two men to each other. Because it assumes reciprocity in the fulfilling of needs, desires, and expectations, it places both partners under shared obligations to treat each other with sensitivity and fairness so that the balance of gains and sacrifices does not tip radically in the direction of only one of them. Because it requires trust it must include confiding and the vulnerability that comes with the personal and material dependency of two people on each other. Because it deals with each partner's expectations for the future, it must allow breathing space for each, room for experimentation, for growth, for individual autonomy of thought and action, for a future that is not a mere duplication of the past. (p. 3)

Finally, Heyward (1984) extends these practical observations about gay/lesbian fidelity, linking the reconceptualization of fidelity to the process of choosing monogamy or nonmonogamy as the framework for our relationships. In so doing, she also synthesizes pragmatism and theological/ethical reflection for us. She agrees, for example, that genuine fidelity in our sexuality is absolutely not "synonymous with monogamy," and argues that, "from a moral perspective, decisions about monogamy can be made responsibly only insofar as we have struggled to know what may be involved in being a faithful friend or lover" (p. 185). The practicalities of "what may be involved" entail both love and commitment; she thus reiterates the findings of the various couples surveys when she says, "Sexual lovers and good friends know that the most compelling relationships demand hard work, patience, and a willingness to endure tensions and anxiety in creating mutually empowering bonds" (pp. 186-187). Living/embodying genuine fidelity, within the practicalities of our everyday lives, also assumes theological and even prophetic qualities. Our lives and relationships, as genuinely faithful lovers, wed theory and praxis, as Heyward (1984) elaborates:

> To be sexually faithful is to experience and express ourselves relationally in such a way that both we and others are empowered, and empowering,

as co-creators, liberators, and bearers of bless-
ing to one another and to the world. To be faithful lovers is to touch and be touched . . . with a
depth and quality of tenderness that actually
helps create life where there is death, comfort
where there is despair. To be faithful in our
sexualities is to live a commitment to mutual, re-
ciprocal relations between and among ourselves in
which no one owns, possesses, dominates, or con-
trols the other but rather in which the lover par-
ticipates with the beloved in living together in a
home, a society, and/or a world in which each
gives and receives. (p. 192)

Whether we choose monogamy or nonmonogamy, as long
as our sexuality is borne of justice, of commitment to
the wholeness and well-being of our partners and ourselves, and of self-acceptance and fundamental gay
pride, then our genuinely faithful sexuality becomes a
prophetic embodiment of liberating, nonpossessive, and
deeply compassionate love (cf., Hay, 1987). Rather
than binding two partners in a possessive genital exclusivity, genuine fidelity actually liberates the in-
dividuals-in-relationship, both for their individual
growth and for their sexually empowered and justice-
seeking participation in the world, as Heyward (1984)
poetically describes:

To say I love you is to say that you are not
mine, but rather your own.
To love you is to advocate your rights, your
space, your self, and to struggle with you, rather
than against you, in our learning to claim our
power in the world.
To love you is to make love to you, and with
you, whether in . . . our common work or play, in
our struggle for social justice, or in the ecstasy
and tenderness of intimate embrace that we believe
is just and right for us--and for others in the
world. (p. 92)

Ultimately, genuine fidelity weaves together the
"potentially profound meaning of genital intercourse
and the divine intention that it be used for human fulfillment most richly defined" (Nelson, 1978, pp. 156-
157). As such, it embraces and embodies our concerns
for mind/body/spirit wholeness and growth for ourselves, our partners, and our relationships. It also
enables a deepened intimacy and communion between two

unique and distinct selves whose coming together sexually can also disclose divine co-presence and co-celebration. Finally, whether monogamously or nonmonogamously, enacting a sexuality borne of genuine fidelity, of love, and of justice can enable us to embrace and to embody a liberating sexuality which stands in prophetic tension with heterosexist models of relationship and which also enables us to explore and create new models of nonpossessive and sexually loving and committed relationship.

* * *

V. Sexual and Relational Models and Alternatives

(i) Befriending our Partners and Lovers

In her presentation during the 1988 meetings of the American Academy of Religion, Plaskow (1988) described the profound, mutually relational force of human sexuality, and of gay/lesbian sexuality in particular, as the "erotic nature of community." Echoing the writings of fellow lesbian/feminist theologian Heyward (1982, 1984), her metaphor reiterated an understanding of sexuality as the empowerment of mutual relationships in a communal quest for justice. For many gay men and lesbians the "erotic nature of community" has assumed multidimensionality most recently in the Names Project, the quilted memorial to the thousands who have died of AIDS. In our participation in local quilting bees, in our experience of viewing over nine acres of quilted memorial panels on the Washington Monument Ellipse in October 1988 and again in 1989, and in our 200,000 candles held aloft to surround the Lincoln Memorial reflecting pool, we have (re)learned the meaning and pathos of erotic and constructed community and/or surrogate family. Gay men in particular have realized that every gay male Names Project volunteer who has offered us a tissue or a comforting hug, that every gay chorus member or fellow leatherman whose life is commemorated in the quilt, and that every other gay man's panel as well, represents someone who could have been a lover, a one-night stand, a friend, a brother.

Our experience of the Names Project has deepened the bonds of erotic community among gay people and intertwined our lives not only with those of the many non-gay sufferers of AIDS and AIDS-related complex (ARC), but with all persons whose lives have been affected by AIDS. For us, the "erotic nature of community" undergirds our shared grief and empowers our communal demand for justice and appropriate response to the health crisis. Together, AIDS and the pathos of erotic community are also leading us to more accurately discern and to more deeply appreciate ways in which we can be genuinely faithful friends and lovers. The urgency of the health crisis and the pathos of community also demand that we (re)evaluate and (re)construct life-affirming paradigms for our relationships.

In an interview prior to his own death from AIDS-related complications, French philosopher Michel Foucault insisted that more than merely accepting our gay/lesbian sexuality, we must "continually construct it" (Gallagher and Wilson, 1987, p. 28). Because homosexuality itself, as well as homosexual behavior and relational patterns, have so often been defined by others in ways which protect heterosexism and heterosexuals, Foucault further argued that for gay people to establish authentic self-hood and relationships, we must continually examine our own potential and create or construct ourselves apart from socially constructed roles (Gallagher and Wilson, 1987). The most rigid roles over against which we must (re)construct our relationships are the gender roles which patriarchy has bequeathed to us (cf., Clark, 1989). Writes Heyward (1984), for example, "The healthiest, most creative homosexual relationships are those in which the women or the men do not . . . simply duplicate, or act out, the very sex roles we have rejected . . . as ill-fitting and disempowering" (p. 195). McNeill (1983) anticipates this observation in his own tender and prophetic remarks specifically to gay men, when he similarly writes, "The [gay male] community is potentially free from the psychological need to establish their male identity by means of violence [and control], . . . reconditioned by their ability to accept and celebrate their sexuality" as the source of other passions (p. 59). Gay men are thus called to enact a new masculinity free of both violence and domination, and to be both symbols and embodiments of a secure male identity without gender roles (cf., McNeill, 1983, Clark, 1989).

Scholarly observers of gay and lesbian couples are in fact discovering that the traditional hetero-monogamous marriage-and-gender-roles model is not the predominant pattern or model for the large majority of actual gay relationships (Harry, 1988, Peplau, 1988). Eschewing male dominance and gender role power structures, gay male relationships, for example, most often follow a "best friends" model instead (DeCecco, 1988, Peplau, 1988). While patriarchy has persistently enculturated men to be directly competitive and inherently suspicious of one another, the subversive and erotic power of gay community--especially in the face of AIDS--is enabling friendship (and hence mutual cooperation) to

deepen as a value and model for gay men and our relationships. Laner (1988) thus reports that gay/lesbian
couples are more equal, honest, and candid with one another than their heterosexual counterparts. Mutual affection and companionship, rather than total needs fulfillment; values consensus and enhanced accuracy in
perceiving one's partner's priorities; and, equality or
shared power in decision-making processes, all together
inform gay/lesbian relationships constructed on the
"best friends" model (Harry, 1988, Laner, 1988, Peplau,
1988, Peplau and Cochran, 1988).

As best friends, gay male partners, for example,
place fewer demands upon one another and interact less
possessively; partners are free to fulfill various
needs and goals through a variety of interrelationships. Peplau (1988) even goes so far as to argue that
the hetero-monogamous demand for sexual exclusivity may
actually work against enduring "best friends" couples;
genuine friendship ideally precludes such genital possessiveness (cf., DeCecco, 1988). As best friends, gay
male partners are also frequently able to transcend age
differences with mutuality and equity. While Harry
(1988), for example, reports that age differences
rather than gender roles sometimes cause power imbal-
ances among gay male partners, he insists from his
findings that age differences do not insure inequality;
friendship can transcend the patriarchally constructed
separations of both gender role and ageist categoriza-
tions.

The most striking feature of the "best friends"
model for gay/lesbian relationships is the extent to
which partners in a gay or lesbian couple are able to
sustain their individual autonomy and shared interdependence while simultaneously recognizing that the relationship itself is a third ontological reality. A
gay or lesbian couple is really a threesome, composed
of the two individual partners and the relationship
they construct, nurture, and sustain together. Consequently, McWhirter and Mattison (1984) argue that "the
relationship needs to be nurtured as if it were a separate entity [while each individual] must continue to
grow and change" (p. 295). The process of nurturing
and sustaining this third entity requires that the
lovers/friends work to achieve an optimal, fluid and
processive balance of various factors. Lee (1988), for
example, speculates that a successful relationship
would entail an optimal blend of erotic attraction and
sexual play, including concern and respect between
partners, and of companionship and long-lasting compat-

ibility, all with a minimum of jealousy, envy, and insecurity. Similarly, McWhirter and Mattison (1988) encourage gay male couples in particular to achieve a
balance of individuation and togetherness, of autonomy
and dependence, of conflict and resolution, and of confusion and understanding. They further imply that the
essential trustworthiness and dependability of the relationship itself, as a solid grounding, actually enables and facilitates the various balancing processes.
Speaking directly to the balance of autonomy and dependence, Peplau and Cochran (1988) add that "attachment
and autonomy are independent dimensions [of a relation-
ship], not polar opposites," not mutually exclusive (p.
201, cf., p. 213).

     Balancing attachment and autonomy can also further
facilitate a couple's efforts to construct nonmonogamy.
Peplau and Cochran (1988) thus argue that balanced
autonomy and dependence needs enable partners to have
outside interests, needs fulfillment, and even sex, in
addition to the primary relationship, and not instead
of what the primary partners provide each other. With
friendship as a primary value for gay men in particular, outside sexual play can ideally include comrade-
ship, trust/respect, and pleasure, along with honesty
about the absence of future commitments (Lee, 1988),
all of which should ideally preclude any dehumanizing
objectification of outside sexual partners (cf., Nelson, 1978).

     Balancing is also a part of developing and sus-
taining intimacy. Balancing vulnerability, self-expo-
sure, and even occasional helplessness, with trust and
risk, much like balancing autonomous engagement in the
world with mutual interdependence, can nurture an optimal level of intimacy (Silverstein, 1981). Silverstein
(1981) does, however, caution us as to the delicate nature of intimacy. Intimacy depends more upon simple,
everyday interactions and gestures than contrived
events or purchased gifts; moreover, while "most of us
want periods of intimacy with our lovers with some fre-
quency and miss these severely when we are deprived,
. . . almost everyone at some point wants to lessen the
intensities of intimacy" (p. 170). Achieving and sustaining an optimal intimacy is thus itself an ongoing
balancing process as well. Speaking again to the issue
of sexual encounters outside a primary relationship,
Silverstein (1981) suggests that such encounters may be
less about sexual gratification in itself and more
about creating/restoring some necessary distance between lovers. Not only can such outside excursions po-

tentially rekindle an eroticism which may have been impaired by too much intimacy (cf., McWhirter and Mattison, 1984), they may in fact restore a more manageable level of intimacy between primary partners, rebalancing autonomy and dependence (Silverstein, 1981). When such outside sexual encounters get too complicated or otherwise threaten the primary relationship, however, we are again reminded that outside sexual activities always risk damaging our primary relationships and/or hurting our primary partners, even though they may also promise certain benefits (see chapter 3, above). Consequently, Silverstein (1981) remarks that "it is ironic that many gay male [couples] break up because of the closeness and intimacy that has developed"--and because of the difficulties of achieving and sustaining optimal, balanced intimacy--"not because men can't become intimate" (p. 187).

That gay men can achieve intimacy, that best-friendship is not only possible between gay men, but is actually the implicit paradigm for many gay male as well as lesbian couples, again reminds us of the subversive and healing potential of the "erotic nature of community," over against patriarchal models. Based on their observations of such couples, Jones and Bates (1988) provide an articulate summary description of couples who are sustaining long term best-friendship:

> Highly successful couples report greater appreciation of the partner and the couple as a unit, less conflict, and more feelings that could contribute to stability, such as positive feelings about love relationships and future plans as a couple. (p. 244)

While best-friendship has thus clearly been an implicit alternative model for gay/lesbian sexual relationships all along, our theological and ethical efforts to explicitly celebrate friendship as a value and a paradigm for purposefully constructing our relationships can now be further enabled by the realization of theological, and even biblical, precedents for this synthesis of sexuality and friendship.[6]

(ii) Exploring Theological Precedents

The subversive potential of same-sex friendships to undermine patriarchal competitiveness and hierarchical separations has led Foucault (Gallagher and Wilson, 1987) to suggest that the so-called problem of homosexuality is not so much a concern over sexual acts as it is a fear of affectional relations which are outside patriarchically normative patterns of control. In his extended interview comments, he has described both the valuation of friendship in antiquity and the demise of friendship as a perceived threat to the final ascendance of patriarchal authority in medieval Christendom:

> For centuries after antiquity, friendship was a very important kind of social relation: a social relation within which people had a certain freedom, a certain kind of choice . . . as well as very intense emotional relations. . . . People were also obliged to help their friends, and so on.
>
> . . . From the sixteenth century on, texts . . . explicitly criticize friendship as something dangerous.
>
> The army, bureaucracy, administration, universities, schools [all the institutional forms of an entrenched patriarchy] cannot function with such intense friendships.
>
> . . . The disappearance of friendship as a social relation and the declaration of homosexuality as a social/political/medical problem are the same process. (Gallagher and Wilson, 1987, pp. 32-33, 34)

In his earlier groundbreaking text, Boswell (1980) reports that ecclesiastical efforts to discourage same-sex friendship began even earlier, with the rise of Thomist Catholicism after the twelfth century. From Thomas Aquinas to the present, Christianity has not only opposed "particular friendships" between same-sex religious, but conveniently suppressed the writings of earlier ecclesiastical advocates of friendship as well. The most important earlier work, for our gay/lesbian theological and ethical reflections, is that of the gay twelfth century saint, Aelred of Rievaulx (1110-1167 CE). Aelred acknowledged his own early homosexual experience and made clear that his decision to enter monastic life was not a rejection of his active homosexual past. Both his interactions with the monks under his charge, as Abbot of Rievaulx, and his "theology of passionate friendship" were clearly colored and informed by his gay perspective (Boswell, 1980, Clark, 1987, Daniel, 1950, Hallier, 1969, Roby, 1974, Russell, 1982, Squire, 1981). As such, Aelred's too long overlooked theology provides an important precedent for our efforts to construct a "best friends" model of loving gay/lesbian sexuality.

Aelred's starting point for a theology of friendship was one with which contemporary gay men and lesbians might also comfortably begin:

> Neither attraction nor reason alone should constitute love [or friendship] but, rather, the conjunction of both. Physical beauty was . . . a completely legitimate inspiration of love. . . . Carnal relationships [although] not desirable for monks . . . did afford the joy felt by lovers, and . . . could be used as stepping-stones to a loftier relationship involving the two lovers and God. (Boswell, 1980, p. 224)

Aelred's authority for such a validation of human relating was none other than Jesus' own befriending of persons, specifically the intimacy of Jesus with the "beloved disciple" John, a relationship which Aelred described as a "perfect love" and a "heavenly marriage" (Boswell, 1980, pp. 225, 226). Three other theological models also supported Aelred's teaching. Not only does the Jesus/John relationship validate friendship, but the relationship of the heavenly Father (sic.) to the Son is another divine model for friendship. The Father/Son relationship provides a model for the intimacy which should exist between friends, while the Trinity provides a model for appropriate community (Hallier, 1969). Finally, Aelred also believed that God's very reason for creating was to love, and be loved by, creation. Consequently, persons within friendships are the truest embodiments of the image of God, and fallenness is the perversion of this inclination toward union with fellow persons and with God (Roby, 1974, Hallier, 1969).

Boswell (1980) is correct, however, when he goes on to point out that Aelred "specifically posited friendship and human love . . . as a means of approaching divine love" (p. 222, emphasis added, cf., Hallier, 1969). Aelred insisted that human love and relationships should always engender love of the divine (Roby, 1974, Squire, 1981). For Aelred, love progressively transforms the soul from being carnal to being spiritual; love seeks a depth of intimacy and spirituality which in turn seeks to transcend the physical. Carnal relationships, gay or non-gay, are merely the lowest stepping-stones, acceptably youthful or immature starting points; carnality must be transcended by mature spiritual friendship and the latter should also be transcended by, or at least lead to, the contemplation of and love for God (Roby, 1974, cf., Hallier, 1969, Squire, 1981, Clark, 1987).

Aelred's apparent sex-negativity must not be understood, however, out of its monastic context; he did not relegate sexually active persons, gay or non-gay, to second-class citizenship as did Paul, Augustine, and others. His own self-acceptance of both his homosexually active youth and his life-long gay feelings precluded that. He was, however, as concerned for his monk's maintaining their vows as for allowing them to develop chaste, same-sex intimacies (Clark, 1987). His challenge to contemporary gay men and lesbians, therefore, would probably focus upon priorities: Sexually active gay people must live paradoxically (and, hence, wholistically) with both their sexuality and their spirituality; Aelred's progression must be conflated and both the love of God and a responsible sexual love rightly ordered. Irresponsible or dehumanizing or impersonal promiscuity is precluded, while a responsible gay orientation is still affirmed. Sexual love, gay or non-gay, should simply facilitate rather than circumvent or distract from communion with the divine in the encounter with another person (Clark, 1987, cf., Russell, 1982).

Given Aelred's gay perspective, his theology of passionate friendship not only challenges us with its theological models and scheme of priorities; it also provides certain valuable guidelines for developing relationships. Friendship, intimate human interrelationship, is an indicator of spiritual health, insofar as God is encountered in sharing with another person. Hence, the desire for friendship is both a natural desire and a virtue (Squire, 1981). Moreover, as a virtue, friendship is not to be sought for any other benefits or consequent advantages. Although good fruits may result from friendship, friendship itself is intrinsically valuable (Roby, 1974). Friendship also requires vulnerability, trust, and emotional risk--qualities only developed over time. Such risked involvement entails genuine, selfless openness to the sufferings and joys, criticism and praise of one's friend, as well as a humble sensitivity to his/her lacks and needs. Intimacy and trust enable prudent, loving criticism of one's friend and an equally patient receptivity to criticism. Thus, neither individual experiences condescension or compelled deference, and both are nurtured in their spiritual growth (Roby, 1974, cf., Clark, 1987).

Aelred also cautioned against too hastily entering into relationships which might prove false. Friends are to be chosen with care and tested with caution. Aelred outlined four stages for the development of a friendship: selection, probation or testing, admission to friendship, and perfect harmony. A potential friend is to be tested (stage two) as to loyalty, right intention, discretion, and patience. One is expected never to violate the trust, confidentiality, and love of one's friend, and always to embody humility and loving forgiveness before one's companion. False friendships, for example, are relationships entered solely for carnal pleasure or for material gain (Roby, 1974, cf., Clark, 1987).

Overall, Aelred was not only able to accept his own homosexuality and to discipline his gay feelings into a saintly love within a celibate, monastic environment; he was also able to draw upon those very emotions to create a theological position which allowed himself and his monks to create and nurture intimate relationships and to love one another deeply. His theological models, scheme of priorities, and guidelines for friendship still challenge us to construct mature, responsible relationships with one another. A friendship and/or sexual relationship is sanctified after the model of Jesus and John, while the two friends are ever to remember that their own intimacy and love and even sexual sharing together create an encounter wherein God also is present. For gay St. Aelred, a human friendship should always direct the two friends toward that ultimate, divine companion (Clark, 1987).

Two other biblical models of importance for our gay/lesbian theological and ethical reflections as to the value of friendship for our sexuality--models which Aelred could also have used--involve Old Testament relationships. The clearly homosexual relationship of David and Jonathan, for example, embodied a friendship not unlike those celebrated in classical Greek legends and myths as an honorable love between two heroic figures (cf., Horner, 1978):

> When he had finished speaking to Saul, the soul of Jonathan was knit to the soul of David, and Jonathan loved him as his own soul. . . . Then Jonathan made a covenant with David, because he loved him as his own soul.

> . . . "When the Lord cuts off every one of
> the enemies of David from the face of the earth,
> let not the name of Jonathan be cut off from the
> house of David. And may the Lord take vengeance
> on David's enemies." And Jonathan made David
> swear again by his love for him; for he loved him
> as he loved his own soul. . . .
> "How are the mighty fallen in the midst of
> the battle!
> "Jonathan lies slain upon thy high places. I
> am distressed for you, my brother Jonathan; very
> pleasant have you been to me; your love to me was
> wonderful, [sur]passing the love of women." (I
> Samuel 18:1,3; 20:15b-17; II Samuel 1:25-26 [RSV])

Similarly, the less explicit relationship between the
widowed Ruth and her mother-in-law Naomi exemplifies an
abiding and self-sacrificial friendship between two
women:

> But Naomi said to her two daughters-in-law, "Go,
> return each of you to her mother's house. May the
> Lord deal kindly with you, as you have dealt with
> the dead and with me."
> . . . But Ruth said, "Entreat me not to leave
> you or to return from following you; for where you
> go I will go, and where you lodge I will lodge;
> your people shall be my people, and your God my
> God; where you die I will die, and there will I be
> buried. May the Lord do so to me and more also if
> even death parts me from you." And when Naomi saw
> that she was determined to go with her, she said
> no more. (Ruth 1:8,15-18 [RSV])

In addition to these two classical Old Testament ex-
amples of the synthesis of same-sex friendship and sexuality, the New Testament figure of Jesus remains as
significant for our contemporary reflections about sexual friendship as it did for St. Aelred eight centuries
ago. In a sense extending Aelred's use of the Jesus
figure as exemplary, Ruether (1978) has provided, for
our purposes, an intriguing in-depth examination of
Jesus and his sexuality in both canonical and noncanonical sources (cf., Clark, 1987, 1989).
Ruether (1978) argues that while the traditional
image of Jesus is one of holiness divorced from sexuality, the most historically reliable layers of the Syn-
optic gospels (Matthew, Mark, and Luke) do not imply
that sexuality is the heart of sinfulness. Jesus him-

self was far more concerned with the "sins of religious hypocrisy [and] the sins of the powerful among the religious and economic elite against the little ones" (p. 134). Indeed, she has discovered the possibility that Jesus' own sexuality was channeled in neither acceptable direction insofar as "he appears to be neither married nor celibate" (p. 135). Unlike Aelred, therefore, she consequently pays equal attention to both Jesus' primary relationships, with Mary Magdalene and with John. Of Mary as portrayed in noncanonical writings, Ruether (1978) says that her "role is affirmed as a way of castigating religious male chauvinism and upholding the equality of women. . . . Jesus is even portrayed as having a special love relationship with Mary Magdalene. She is his beloved disciple. She understands him better than the others, and he responds with physical caresses" (p. 135). Equally clear within the canon, Jesus' relation to John was also one of love which included physical touching and signs of affection. John is "repeatedly referred to as the one who laid his head on Jesus' breast" (p. 136). Ruether (1978) uses this bisexual potential within the person of Jesus as a standpoint for criticizing patriarchal machismo:

> There is much in the model of Jesus in the New Testament which makes him decidedly a male who was, if not unmasculine, at least iconoclastic toward male models of power and authority.
>   . . . The striking fact about the Synoptics is the lack of [sex-role] stereotyping. . . . His is an authority that overthrows conventional models of patriarchal, hierarchical, religious, and political power systems; that champions women, the poor, the . . . outcasts [and] that rejects the power games of the male leadership classes. (p. 136)

Ruether's (1978) conclusions thus appropriately criticize the patriarchal obsession with sexuality, while simultaneously elucidating Jesus' own proper prioritizing of sexuality:

> Jesus' life gives no exclusive sanctification to a particular sexual lifestyle, whether celibate or married, hetero- or homosexual, as the normative model. . . . None of these options is enshrined, none is ruled out. . . .

> If there is anything at all to be said about
> the sexuality of Jesus it is that it was a sexual-
> ity under the control of friendship. He could
> love both John and Mary Magdalene, physically em-
> brace and be embraced by them, because first of
> all he knew them as friends, not as sexual ob-
> jects. (p. 137, emphases added)

While no real evidence either for sexual activity or
for its particular absence (celibacy) exists per se in
the sources and texts, the picture which does emerge is
that of a Jesus who was not obsessed with sexuality,
but who instead was able to relate intimately, ten-
derly, and equally with both men and women in ways
which also included physical affection and in ways always guided by friendship and not by sexual objectification or exploitation (cf., Clark, 1987, 1989). Jesus
was, according to Ruether (1978), a fully sexual (and
probably actively sexual) individual whose relationships were nevertheless "controlled not by sexuality,
but by friendship" (p. 137). That priority can be a
part of his exemplary force for our gay/lesbian theological and ethical activity, insofar as we seek to affirm and to celebrate our sexuality in responsible and
compassionate ways as lesbians and gay men, in the very
face of AIDS, while also responding to both our sick
and our well friends as friends first and not just as
sexual objects (Clark, 1989).

(iii) Transcending the Coupled Paradigm

The (com)passionate disclosure of the divine in
loving and orgasmic gay sexuality implicit in St. Aelred's theology, the heroic love of Jonathan and David,
the self-sacrificial love of Ruth and Naomi, and the
bisexually informed friendships of Jesus with both Mary
Magdalene and John, all of these theological precedents
reaffirm for us the value of friendship as a paradigm
for gay/lesbian sexuality and relationships.   Importantly, none of these precedents is primarily informed
by hetero-monogamous romantic love, by gender roles restrictions, or by either genital exclusivity or sexual
obsession. Our theological and ethical reflections are
thereby prompted to reexamine our discourse regarding
monogamy and nonmonogamy: While our discussion of
these options thus far risks presuming that coupling is
itself a primary goal for all gay/lesbian interrelationships, both our theological precedents and the realities of the sexual permutations of gay/lesbian life

call into question the universalizability of the coupling paradigm for us. At the very least, to focus strictly on monogamy/nonmonogamy and the advantages and disadvantages of each risks overlooking the fact, as Foucault has reminded us in another interview (Barbadette, 1982), that "the single person must be recognized as having relations with others that are quite different from those of a . . . couple" (p. 38). If we are able, therefore, to shift our discourse from romantic notions of coupling to the already implicit valuation of friendship for our gay/lesbian sexuality, our reflective movement from exploring monogamy/nonmonogamy, to articulating a broader understanding of what it means to be genuinely faithful in our sexualities, can now open still further to explore the richer spectrum and liberational potential of a variety of sexually relational forms. As Foucault again reminds us, "We have to understand that . . . through our desires, go new forms of relationships, new forms of love, new forms of creation. [Sexuality] is a possibility for creative life" (Gallagher and Wilson, 1987, p. 28).

In at least two interviews with the gay press in the years just prior to his death (Barbadette, 1982, Gallagher and Wilson, 1987), Foucault adamantly insisted that discourse about homosexuality should shift from a focus on sexual behavior toward a discovery of new relational forms. Gay freedom from procreative necessities and gender roles, gay sexual empowerment, and our (re)valuation of friendship, can together liberate us from the monogamy (coupled)/nonmonogamy (single) dualism which, inherited from patriarchy, still infuses our community. Arguing that "we live in a legal, social, and institutional world where the only relations possible are extremely few, extremely simplified, and extremely poor," he urges the gay/lesbian community to "imagine and create . . . new relational right[s] which [permit] all possible types of relations to exist and not be prevented, blocked, or annulled by impoverished relational institutions" (Barbadette, 1982, p. 38). Just as he recognized the danger which friendships posed for historically developing patriarchal systems of control (Gallagher and Wilson, 1987), he also understood that "society and the institutions which frame it have limited the possibility[ies] of relationships because a rich relational world would be very complex to manage"; he nevertheless admonishes the gay/lesbian community to be at the forefront of fighting against "this shrinking of the relational fabric" (Barbadette, 1982, p. 38).

Consequently, as might well be expected, Foucault has consistently criticized simplistic and/or unreflective adaptations of hetero-monogamous, marriage-style coupling as a paradigm for gay/lesbian relationships:

> If you ask people to reproduce the marriage bond for their personal relationship to be recognized, the progress made is slight.
> . . . To use the model of [monogamous/nuclear] family life, or the institution of the family, for . . . this kind of friendship would be quite contradictory. (Barbadette, 1982, p. 38, Gallagher and Wilson, 1987, p. 34)

Instead of simplistic imitation, Foucault would advocate a more reflective and purposive exploration and construction of relational forms which will more authentically support a sexuality of friendship. The real task for gay men and lesbians becomes that of creating new social and relational forms, values, and structures:

> I think that there is an interesting [role for the gay/lesbian culture] to play. . . . I mean culture in the large sense, a culture which invents ways of relating, types of existence, types of values, types of exchanges between individuals that are really new and are neither the same as, nor superimposed on, existing cultural forms. . . . Let's escape as much as possible from the type of relations which society proposes for us and try to create in the empty space where we are new relational possibilities. (Barbadette, 1982, p. 39)

In his own recent efforts to begin discovering and/or creating new "types of values" and new "types of exchanges" for gay/lesbian sexuality, McNeill (1988) has attempted to reintegrate sexuality and human playfulness. He thus insists not only that "the sex drive is the physical dimension of a human need to escape isolation and alienation for a profound physical and spiritual unity," but also that "intimacy, both physical and spiritual, is precisely the goal of playful sex" (p. 132, cf., Heyward, 1984). Echoing St. Aelred, McNeill (1988) concludes that "a loving, playful sexual encounter can become the locus of a mystical experience of the divine" (p. 136). He even goes so far as to celebrate the observation that "at its best, the gay sexual revolution freed sexual expression from all ar-

tificial restraints and restored it to its proper human
context of joyous play" (p. 134).

By revaluing and reintegrating "joyous play" with
our gay/lesbian sexuality in his pastoral reflections,
McNeill (1988) also reminds us that playfulness requires friendship and mutuality while it precludes objectifying or trivializing our partners: "Healthy,
playful human sex requires that the sex partners treat
each other as end in themselves; a failure to do so re-
duces one's partner to [a mere] object," to a utilitarian (used/exploited) tool in pursuit of one's own
self-centered pleasure, thereby making sex work and not
genuine play (p. 131). In other words, to (re)value
play as an important aspect of our gay/lesbian sexuality enables us to reclaim both the intrinsic value and
the inherent joy both of mutual friendship (St. Aelred)
and of our very sexuality itself (cf., Clark, 1989,
Doustourian, 1978, Heyward, 1984). The creativity and
utter mutuality inherent in play can help insure our
sexual interactions against both the body/spirit and
self/other alienation, and the genitally focused utili-
tarianism, of patriarchal models for human sexuality.
McNeill (1988) elaborates:

> The first condition necessary for play is that the
> human activity must be meaningful in itself and
> not be related to a goal that lies beyond the
> playful action itself; it must be totally meaning-
> ful here and now.
>   . . . If it is impossible for us to live
> fully in the present moment, then we will never be
> able to be present fully for another person. The
> ability to do so . . . to be fully present for an-
> other, is probably the primary reason why, when we
> succeed in playing, we experience such intense joy
> and fulfillment.
>   . . . Some of that freedom to play comes from
> [accepting our] exiled status. We are frequently
> no longer involved in competing. As a result,
> lesbians and gays are much freer . . . to engage
> in activities for their own sake. (p. 117, em-
> phases added)

Our various theological precedents, Michel Foucault's prophetic words, and McNeill's (1988) reflections on sexual play, taken altogether, strongly suggest that our gay/lesbian theology and ethics should be
about the business not only of affirming the fundamental and intrinsic goodness of our sexuality, but also

of (re)valuing and promoting friendship/mutuality/com-
munity as the broadest and healthiest paradigm for our
sexual interrelationships. Appreciating the "erotic
nature of community" (Plaskow, 1988), alongside revaluing both playfulness and friendship in the age of AIDS,
can open us to the fully liberational power, depth, and
joy inherent in our capacities for developing just mutual relationships. On the one hand, gay/lesbian
couples can authentically choose to construct monogamous relationships which do not merely imitate hetero-
monogamy--which are constructed not on gender roles
and/or genital possessiveness, but on playful and loving friendship, equality, mutual interdependence, and
openness to full sociopolitical participation both
within the gay subculture and in the world (cf.,
DeCecco, 1988, Marcus, 1988, Uhrig, 1984). On the
other hand, nonmonogamous primary couples, as well as
single gay men and lesbians, can both affirm, respect,
and honor the value of those monogamous couples and
share in their quests for appropriate legal protections
and social structures, while simultaneously exploring a
plethora of other options.

     Nonmonogamous couples, for example, must continue
to work out an appropriate balancing of priorities,
neither undermining their primary relationships nor dehumanizing their outside sexual partners. Revaluing
friendship holds the potential for enabling lovers to
be "best friends" in unpossessive and undemanding ways
--thus helping to diffuse jealousy, envy, and low self-
esteem--while also allowing friendship to inform all
outside sexual interactions as well. With consistent
adherence to safe-sex practices, single gay men (and
lesbians) are freed from societal and peer pressure to
become coupled and are thereby also freed to construct
friendship networks and surrogate families wherein
love, affection, and play can be expressed sexually.
With friendship as an absolute value and paradigm for
our sexuality, we can at long last disabuse ourselves
of the wrongheaded notion that intimate and/or long-
standing friendship precludes sexual expression and/or
that sexual expression must always be novel, between
strangers (the "but we can't sleep together, we're
sisters!" syndrome). Moreover, we are also called to
infuse even our one-night stands with compassionate befriending, as well as with playfulness, and also with
subsequent respect and compassion. And, finally, as
Mendola (1980) has counseled us, our uncouplings now
become occasions for transforming the nature of our
love as couples to that of nurturant friendship,

thereby better enabling our solitary embarking through the changes requisite for becoming single again.

Whereas the coupling paradigm has frequently been too narrow, creating dualisms of monogamy/nonmonogamy and of us (the politely coupled) vs. them (the presumably promiscuous), the paradigm of friendship embraces a liberational spectrum of relational forms and possibilities. It provides a primary and humanizing value for all of our sexual encounters and encourages us to explore and to construct various forms of relationship that can be idiosyncratically appropriate and authentic for us. We (re)learn the fluid, processive, and even playful nature of human interpersonal relationships--apart from misleading and rigid patriarchal patterns of control--and (re)discover the depth and wonder, pathos and empowerment of erotic liberational community. Our sexual/relational variety and our mutual quest(s) for sociopolitical justice become fully informed by the value of friendship. Not surprisingly, the more radical aspects and potentials of the friendship paradigm for gay/lesbian sexuality are already being explored and enacted within sub-groups of the gay community themselves often considered too extreme by many "mainstream" gay men and lesbians. The distinct but overlapping arenas of leathersex and S/M, for example, enable radical sexual experimentation, or play, and deeply (com)passionate interrelationships perhaps only possible at the extreme margins of patriarchal acceptability. Leathersex and S/M, particularly as these spaces facilitate alternatives to patriarchal sexual paradigms, also deserve gay/lesbian theological and ethical reflection, therefore, in order for us to move toward defiantly inclusive celebration of the full spectrum of gay/lesbian sexuality and, ultimately, of all human sexuality.

*   *   *

VI. Radical Sexuality: Leathersex and S/M

(i) Some Conflicting Perspectives

The larger gay/lesbian community is frequently ambivalent in its feelings toward the sub-communities of
gay men and lesbians who identify themselves with
either leathersex, sadomasochism (S/M), or both. Many
so-called assimilationist gays, for example, are as embarrassed by men and women in leather as they are by
transvestites or "drag queens"; they fear that any public visibility on the part of people so completely and
extremely at odds with acceptable heterosexist values
and styles will somehow damage the public perception of
all gay people and/or undermine ongoing efforts at
steady sociopolitical reform within the present patriarchal system. The leathersex and S/M subpopulation(s)
have consequently experienced additional marginalization and disdain, not only from heterosexual society
but from other gay people as well. Resulting misconceptions often include beliefs that leather identity
and participation in S/M are always synonymous, that
only gay men participate in leathersex or S/M, and that
such participation is always cruelly over-masculinized
and self-centered. An underlying misunderstanding is
equally clear--that leathersex and S/M are presumably
misogynist and inhumane, that leathersex or S/M and
compassionate love and/or justice-seeking are mutually
exclusive. Thus, although Collins (1979) has reminded
us that "nothing that is of us can be alien to our theology" (p. 152), that leathersex, and even S/M, might
hold positive significance for gay/lesbian sensibility
and spirituality, theology, or ethics, has frequently
been dismissed as absurd.[7]
Although they do overlap considerably, leather
identity and participation in S/M activities actually
constitute two distinct areas of sexual identity and
interaction (cf., Mains, 1984). Furthermore, a growing
number of women are participating in both arenas of gay
life, and leather and S/M social clubs and events within the gay community increasingly include both men and

women as participants. Even more importantly, these men and women are usually highly compassionate, frequently as tender as they are passionate with their sexual partners, and capable of developing very strong bonds of friendship, or siblinghood, not only among themselves but on behalf of the whole gay/lesbian community. As members of an extreme sub-community built upon absolute trust as well as utter vulnerability, they are both advocates of sociopolitical advances and active fund-raisers and care-givers during the current AIDS health crisis (and many of their eroto-sexual activities are inherently safe-sex). Many of the participants in leathersex and/or S/M thus embody and enact the "erotic nature of community" (Plaskow, 1988). Nevertheless, the combination of ambivalent feelings, of various misconceptions, and, frequently, of simple misunderstanding or lack of knowledge, together sustains an ongoing debate between the critics and the defenders of leathersex and/or S/M, a debate which is thus far primarily addressed to gay male participants.

A major criticism directed at both the leathersex and S/M sub-communities concerns the extent to which attire, attitudes, and symbols, as well as sexual behavior, together reflect and/or reinforce patriarchy and its attendant dualisms. Nelson (1978), for example, believes that even between two consenting partners, both of whom ultimately receive pleasure and fulfillment, S/M "suggests the reinforcement of patterns of psychic body-self alienation" (p. 177). He is concerned that participants in such sexual activity necessarily use sex or compensatory sexual release as a "tool" to balance psyche, as if bodiliness (sexuality) and psyche (spirituality) were dualistic opposites rather than a unity. Likewise, Evans (1988) believes that leathersex revalues machismo to such an extent that things and persons deemed too feminine or "not butch enough" become objects of disdain, thereby reinforcing another dualism, that of polarized gender identity and its related valuations. Finally, Goodman, et al. (1983), decry the domination/submission dualism which they believe leathersex and S/M also reinforce:

> The symbolism is pretty clear [suggesting] that S/M is in fact an expression of the patriarchal connection of masculine power/domination with sexuality. . . . Even though it is voluntary, the sexual acting out of domination/submission accompanied by the infliction of pain seems an intimate

re-run of the daily oppression experienced in a patriarchal society. (p. 106)

That leathersex identity, and particularly S/M activity, thus appear to unwittingly appropriate and re-enact patriarchal dualisms and oppression--among the oppressed themselves--has led Evans (1988) to another critical perspective, one which links leathersex and S/M to internalized homophobia. He suggests early on that "to eroticize the infliction of punishment" on oneself or on one's sexual partners is "a phenomenon that often appears when people feel guilty about their sexual behavior" or about their sexuality in general (p. 126). As a result, when he later concedes that "at their best, lesbians and gay men have dramatically challenged the sexist role-playing that is at the very heart of the patriarchal psychosis and have succeeded in making an immense improvement in the quality of [gay/lesbian] life," he very quickly adds that, "the movement has also had its weaknesses, in particular the tendency of many gay men to internalize self-destructive fantasies of patriarchal masculinity" (p. 183). Excluding lesbians altogether from leathersex and/or S/M, Evans (1988) views these arenas of sexual identity and activity not as defiant celebrations of gay extremity, but only as enactments of gay self-oppression:

> Many gay men have . . . internalized homophobic values. . . . They . . . display intense self-hatred in their sexual practices. . . . A significant minority of present-day American gay men become sexually aroused by the fantasy of hurting, or being hurt by, their sexual partners. In effect, they use sex as a kind of punishment by mutual consent, punishing both themselves and others for being gay. This eroticizing of self-hatred is evidenced in . . . domination, bondage, humiliation, and even torture. . . . So intense is their self-deprecation that they have fallen in love with the image of their worst homophobic oppressors. (p. 179)

All too obviously, the homophobia which permeates western society and culture, particularly in the wake of AIDS, continues to reinforce self-oppressive attitudes and behaviors throughout the whole lesbian/gay community(ies). Just as clearly, the sub-communities of leathersex and S/M participants are not immune to the effects of homophobia; some gay men and lesbians within these communities naturally retain some internalized and unresolved homophobia. Moreover, given the extremity of some S/M activities, the potential for abusing oneself or one's partner(s) is high, particularly when participants unreflectively act out any internalized negative messages, whether internalized homophobia, unresolved childhood abuse and/or neglect, or any other unresolved psychological trauma. Nevertheless, Evans' (1988) sweeping generalization is simply unfounded. He emotively lumps together the remasculinization of some portions of the post-Stonewall gay male community (the "clone" look, as opposed to more androgynous styles) with leathersex and S/M. In so doing, he equates all of these with an implicit gay endorsement of homophobic patriarchy and utterly fails to appreciate the phenomenological reality that the psycho-spiritual experiences of both leathersex and S/M are often cathartically healing processes which move through masculine symbolization, shattering patriarchal restraints in order to approach ecstasy (cf., Mains, 1984, 1987). Similarly, both Evans (1988) and Goodman, et al. (1983), misread the masculinity in leathersex and S/M. Not only do they overlook lesbian participants, some of whom appropriate highly feminine Victorian leather and S/M accessories and behavior, but they also fail to see that leathersex and S/M are "a different phenomenon from cult masculinity" (Silverstein, 1981, p. 230).

In fact, the overly masculinized appearance of gay male leathersex and/or S/M participants can serve some very healthy functions. For many gay men, whose very male identity was undermined in childhood and adolescence by taunts from family and peers who already began to perceive their emerging difference (as "bookworms," nonathletes, class sissies), such remasculinization can help heal old wounds and enable a reintegration of one's identity both as a man and as a gay person (cf., Mains, 1984). Moreover, the symbolization of leathersex masculinity can be just as powerful a parody or satire of patriarchal and hierarchical masculinity as is transvestism (cf., Mains, 1984). As gay men consigned to traditionally female occupations (secretaries and clerks, teachers and counselors, hair dressers and florists) join doctors, lawyers, mechanics, carpenters and other traditionally masculine professionals in self-consciously appropriating the equalizing costumes of leathersex or S/M, their non-hierarchical and democratic extremity bears a kinship with the exaggerated

extremity of some transvestism. Either extreme can undermine patriarchally gender-polarized expectations!

Again in his gay press interviews, Foucault has
addressed some of these issues: While he realizes that
constructing a one-dimensional identity around leathersex and/or S/M can lead "back to a kind of ethics very
close to the old heterosexual virility," he insists
that constructing a multi-dimensional and authentic
gayself identity, instead, one which simply includes
leathersex and/or S/M as one aspect of that identity,
is quite a different matter (Gallagher and Wilson,
1987, p. 31). On its positive side, the remasculinization which leathersex permits gay men not only challenges patriarchy and patriarchal masculinity, but
actually further facilitates a movement beyond pederas-
tically or gender-role constructed relationships toward
a radical (re)affirmation of the equality of love between adult men:

> I think in the schema of a [gay] man affirming
> himself as a man there is a movement toward re-
> defining [which] consists of saying: "Yes, we
> spend our time with men, we have moustaches, and
> we kiss each other," without one of the partners
> having to play the nelly, or the effeminate, fra-
> gile boy.
>   . . . This is all very new and practically
> unknown in Western societies. The Greeks [for ex-
> ample] never admitted love between two adult men.
> (Barbadette, 1982, p. 41)

Ultimately, Foucault's appraisal of leathersex,
and particularly S/M, expands our gay/lesbian theological and ethical examination of these forms of radical
sexuality, thereby enabling us to articulate some re-
sponses which address the various critical viewpoints:
To insist that leathersex or S/M necessarily polarizes
sexuality (body) and psyche (spirit) unfairly belittles
both the sensibilities of any two co-equal participants
and the potential wholism of their shared experience;
to see only domination/submission fails to acknowledge
that the, sometimes interchangeable, roles played out
in sexual activities often give way to mutually reci-
procal and balanced daily relationships; to focus
solely on masculine symbolization overlooks the equality, respect, cooperation, and shared (sub-)community
involvement of both lesbians and gay men within these
overlapping sub-communities; and finally, to label
leathersex and S/M homophobic undercuts their power to

parody and to heal. Leathersex and S/M are not so much
about remasculinization and/or patriarchal enactments
of violence and self-hatred, as they are efforts to
construct new forms of relationship and pleasure (or
"play"). Foucault again elaborates:

> I don't think this movement of sexual practices
> has anything to do with the disclosure or the un-
> covering of S/M tendencies. . . . I think S/M is
> much more than that; it's the real creation of new
> possibilities of pleasure. . . . The idea that S/M
> is related to a deep violence, that S/M practice
> is a way of liberating this violence, this [mascu-
> line/patriarchal] aggression, is stupid. We know
> very well what all those people are doing is not
> aggressive; they are inventing new possibilities
> of pleasure with strange parts of their body--
> through the eroticization of the [whole] body. I
> think it's a kind of . . . creative enterprise,
> which has as one of its main features what I call
> the desexualization of pleasure. (Gallagher and
> Wilson, 1987, p. 30)

In other words, rather than reinforcing a patriarchal dualism of genital sexuality vs. psyche/spirit,
leathersex and S/M activities hold the potential for
ultimately decentering (sexual) pleasure; rather than
focusing upon genital expression and orgasm, they can
encourage and facilitate a playful whole-body eroticism, a pleasuring which integrates body and soul.
Thus with Foucault, our gay/lesbian ethical analysis of
leathersex and S/M not only circumvents certain standard criticism, but begins to move beyond simplistic
understandings, misconceptions, or prejudices about
these arenas of gay/lesbian life, and toward reconceptualization. A complete (re)understanding and (re)con-
ceptualization of the dynamics and meanings of leathersex and S/M may therefore enable us more fully to include them in our defiant celebration.

(ii) An Alternative (Re)conceptualization

While numerous writers have addressed leathersex
and S/M in a variety of forms and media--in gay porno-
graphy and other subcultural publications, such as
Drummer magazine, as well as in very carefully written
"how-to" manuals which inform and guide both the genuinely inquisitive as well as the pruriently curious
(cf., Townsend, 1983)--only one writer to date has pro-

vided an astute and thoroughgoing study of both leathersex and S/M. Mains (1984, 1987) integrates phenomenological observation and philosophical reflection,
physiological knowledge and psychological wisdom, in
order to (re)understand and (re)value the breadth and
depth of these particular forms of radical sexuality,
specifically for gay men. Pondering the curiosity of
the disproportionate number of former clergy who participate in the rituals and passion of leathersex and/or
S/M, he is foremost aware that participants often report that an element of the holy, or the numinous, permeates the dynamics of these overlapping, radically
sexual "spaces," a finding which he summarily explains:

> Trance and catharsis define a form of shared men-
> tal [or psychic] territory in affirming what are
> perhaps some fundamental human qualities--the need
> to give oneself fully and in trust, the need to
> approach and respect one's [physical/psychic/spi-
> ritual] limits as part of self-realization, and
> the need to fully live the human animal. (1984, p.
> 141, 1987, p. 113)

Reiterating that leathersex need not and should not be
reduced to only S/M (1984), he goes on to indicate
that, as a ritualistic wrestling with/pushing against
the limitations of bodiliness, S/M activities in particular can simultaneously and wholistically yield both a
psycho-spiritual and a bio-physical release. Absolutely not gnostically anti-body, therefore, S/M pushes
and expands one's physiological limits to the point
where the "apparently" painful becomes cathartic release, or pleasure instead, thus providing a mental/
psychic/spiritual "euphoria at the edge of physical
limits" (1987, p. 110, cf., pp. 106-111). Even more
importantly, the intimate, shared communication and
trust required of two participants to best facilitate
this process ideally also deepens their interpersonal
and spiritual bonding (cf., 1984).
    The numinous power of entrusting one's physical
and psychic vulnerability to another is evident in a
number of specific activities which Mains (1987) includes within leathersex and S/M (bondage, domination/
submission, "fisting," pain/pleasure, "water sports").
He is quick to add that dominance/submission are not
universal to either leathersex or S/M; in fact, many
participants engage in sexual activities without sexual
role play or with interchangeable roles. Moreover,
when domination/submission are involved, submission is

never involuntary, but is something "given in trust and received voluntarily . . . tempered by an understanding of limits . . . with humility and love. . . . Arrogance and insensitivity have little place" (p. 102). He similarly emphasizes the extent to which utter trust, respect, and intimacy are absolute requirements for an activity such as "fisting," which involves encountering the very "frontier between life and death," insofar as one participant literally holds the entrusted life of the other in his hand (p. 111). Over and over again he reminds us of the profound depths of trust, respect, intimacy, and self-giving love, as well as the finely attuned levels of communication, which healthy wholistic leathersex and S/M both require and facilitate. At their best, both realms of activity also require genuine humility, learned by coming to understand one's own as well as one's partner's limits, and both realms honor emotional warmth and reject any lack of responsive restraint. As a result, the bonding power of these attributes can ideally shape numinously enhanced and deeply loving friendships of (em)power(ment) and (com)passion.

Mains (1984) is also aware that not only do leathersex and S/M balance vulnerability and sensitivity/trust, they also penetrate and reconcile the taboo opposites associated with bodily functions ("water sports"/orgasm; feces/anal intercourse and "fisting"). He implies that, as such, leathersex has the potential for a radical reclamation and reconciliation of body and spirit. As further support for such potential wholism, he similarly emphasizes the extent to which leathersex and S/M also balance our human nature and our animal instincts:

> Vital to self-acceptance, and central to the leather mythos is a reconciliation of the human and the animal.
>   . . . Leather crosses the barriers of cultural sanction to re-embrace animal instincts. But it does so in ways that link the animal with vital human qualities: emotion, symbol, and well-being. (pp. 29, 121)

Far from animalistic, therefore, leathersex and S/M assume archetypal (numinous/mythic) balancing and reconciling functions, not only of risk/trust, but also of instinct/(com)passion, bodiliness/psyche (or spirit), and even life/death, together integrating and creating

a wholistic and relationally enhancing experience between and among participants.

Equally aware that all of his readership may not
have an experiential knowledge of leathersex or S/M,
Mains (1984, 1987) also reviews the processes and by-
products of these sexual interactions to enable a
clearer understanding of their numinous and wholistic
potential. Leathersex and S/M involve actions which
radically disrupt ordinary reality and which "direct
the mind away from the outside world and create a
heightened awareness of the body, its limits, and its
instincts" (1987, p. 105). By so directing the psyche,
"the mind relaxes into and enjoys repressed or hidden
capacities [and] the exercise of fantasy. . . . Fears
and inhibitions are abandoned" (1987, p. 105). Ultimately, dayworld activities and socially constructed
restraints are "replaced with a world of utmost relia-
bility . . . strong personal intimacy . . . trust and
care" (1987, p. 106). Consequently, while the playful
exchanges of leathersex and S/M are intrinsically valuable, fulfilling, and pleasurable for their participants, there are nevertheless at least three significant by-products of such encounters: Self-definition
can accrue through confrontation with one's personal,
psychological, and physical limits, including confronting and resolving one's inhibitions and emotional
conflicts (1984, p. 140, 1987, p. 112). The psychic or
mental state shifts, with such "strong spiritual qualities," can also yield catharsis and emotional release
(1984, p. 140, 1987, p. 113). Building upon the interdependence of physiological neurochemicals to so raise
the pain/pleasure threshold as to "convert" pain to
ecstasy, S/M in particular ideally enables a catharsis
which expunges frustration, guilt, low self-esteem, and
repressed emotions and, consequently, provides new
self-perspective (transcendence), renewed energy for
meeting daily challenges, and a deepening of entrusted
interpersonal bonding. The most important by-product,
therefore, is the strong sense of spiritual and social
comradery, or community, which often develops among
leathersex and S/M participants: "[Individuals] who
have put their lives on the line for their partners
share a special attachment to those who would do the
same" (1984, p. 140f, 1987, p. 113).

That the depths of trust and respect can yield
strong senses of compassion and caring--a deep appreciation of the "erotic nature of community" (Plaskow,
1988)--within this subpopulation of gay men and lesbians is also the linking motivation for the leather

and S/M sub-communities' involvement in larger gay/lesbian community activism, particularly in AIDS support fund-raising and care-giving activities during the current health crisis. Mains (1984), for example, argues that leather is a radical, defiant symbol of gayself-acceptance at the very extremes of socio-sexual marginalization, and that many of the men and women of leather are therefore strongly committed to gay liberation issues: They "share a strong sense of community" (p. 22) and they are "strongly libertarian and share an opposition to injustice" (p. 23). Importantly, "despite the symbolic use of domination and submission within [some of] the rituals of the culture, the leather community is fundamentally egalitarian and fraternal [sic.]," stressing the importance of mutually "contractual approaches between all people" (pp. 30, 83, emphasis added). In fact, ritualized eroto-sexual play through to catharsis diffuses power needs, creating thereby a psycho-spiritual resistance to power abuses (injustice) in the real world. Ritualized leathersex and S/M activities can actually shift power issues (dominance and submission, power and pain) from the unreflective realms of social interactions and power hierarchies into a controlled arena, shattering the facades of everyday power abuses. Whereas daily activities are shaped by traditional social, familial, and business demands which create tensions and frustrations, leathersex and S/M can potentially diffuse and exorcise these tensions. Having fewer power needs in daily life as a result, and a "strong sense of equality and mutual respect" instead, leathersex and S/M participants also frequently share a distrust of "powerseeking in others" (pp. 33, 74).

Mains (1984) finally applies this same analysis to gender roles as well, anticipating criticism like that of Evans (1988) and others, above. Leathersex and/or S/M identity provides one potential means for its gay male participants to begin to redefine masculinity for themselves in liberational forms, simultaneously reclaiming disparaged or "battered" masculinity while parodying cultural constructs of masculinity. As such, leathersex and/or S/M identity need not preclude, but may in fact nurture, a disdain for gender roles and an appreciation of feminist/non-sexist goals. The occasional, conscious appropriation and use of sometimes interchangeable roles in sexual activity can provide a way to see through, penetrate, and break down destructive roles in real life, essentially turning them "inside-out" (cf., p. 73).

Overall then, far from being a negative or embarrassing side of gay and lesbian life, leathersex and/or S/M identity at their most wholistic and healthy levels of enactment and interaction can actually provide models of equality and respect, of the balanced integration of sexuality (bodiliness and animal instincts) and transcendence (psyche and spirituality), and of playful, ritualized catharsis which converts individually repressed emotions into communal liberational empowerment. Moreover, many of the participants in these overlapping erotic sub-communities approach an intimacy with the numinous, or the divine, through the entrusted and deepened bonding of genuine sexual/spiritual friendships, friendships which certainly merit our inclusive gay/lesbian ethical and theological celebration!

* * *

VII. Epilogue: A Celebration

Now that we have traveled through the detailed landscape of our sexuality, we at last approach a clearing which is prepared for our defiant celebration. The fires are freshly lit to banish patriarchal darkness and to invite the moon; impish Pan strokes his wispy goatee and frenzied Dionysus shakes loose his mane-like hair; the spirited daughters of Lesbos link arm-in-arm with befeathered berdaches, as other dancers don their animal skins and the masks of David and Jonathan, of Ruth, Naomi, and Sappho, of Zeus and Ganymede, and even of Jesus and John; still others gather their tambourines and faerie wands as the musicians tune their instruments--all gathered together in this magical cosmic place. The circle forms, inviting and welcoming us to join. And yet, to approach this place pungent with our numinous sexuality humbles us--we hold back as much in fear and awe as overcome by joy. To weave together the provisional strands of our gay/lesbian theological and ethical reflections in order to move even tentatively toward our long awaited sexual celebration is no meager task. Awe-filled, trembling with both our boundless joy and our but newly discovered power, we nevertheless move forward, toward the warmth of our brothers and sisters, and the enspiritment of timbrel and dance, of music and gentle firelight. . . . And the celebration begins!

*   *   *

To approach a celebration of gay/lesbian identity and sexuality by means of theological and ethical reflection is indeed humbling. To transpose the modest particularity of one's personal explorations and the terrain of one's inner world into a public dialogue is certainly to know the provisional nature of every assertion and, at the same time, to test the trustworthiness of one's but tentatively forming conclusions (cf., Rubenstein, 1966, Nelson, 1978). It is to reiterate Morton's (1985) qualification of and invitation to theology-as-activity: "This is how it is with me. How is it with you" (p. xxv)? For me, these explorations disclose similarities in patterns of discourse which suggest some fairly dependable ground. To affirm with Nelson (1978), for example, that morally sound sexual behavior involves our accountability even more than our sexual acts per se, all "in accord with an ethics of love" (p. 198), becomes most meaningful when we understand our capacities for sexual love as our drive toward mutuality and justice-making (Heyward, 1984). Moreover, a genuinely mutuality-creating and justice-seeking gay/lesbian sexuality can best be facilitated by a paradigm of loving and playful friendship, of community and wholeness.

One of the prophetic challenges of our sexuality lies, in fact, in its alchemical power to reconcile opposites, to create wholeness. We must absolutely refuse to separate our genital experience from our spirituality and our sociopolitical interactions in the world. After all, if being gay was really nothing more than a matter of genital logistics and functions, homosexuality would not be so threatening to heterosexist patriarchy. Instead, we know that male homosexuality in particular "threatens to bring down the sacred canopy of an economic, sexual, and racial order founded on the assumption that the 'real man' is a disembodied, dispassionate agency of control" (Heyward, 1984, pp. 198). What we have also learned along the way is that the radical power of genuine interrelationships, in and through sexual expression, creates non-hierarchical friendships and therein discloses divine companionship and advocacy to us. We can in turn use the radical empowerment of who we are as an erotic community of friends (cf., Plaskow, 1988) to explore and to create new relational forms, to challenge all social and ecological forms of injustice, and to embody and enact (or incarnate) models of utter human wholeness and compassion. Our sexuality/self-hood/spirituality, as a unity, is the very source of our spiritual power (cf. Heyward, 1984). Our playful and deeply (com)passionate gay/lesbian sexuality is both a reflection and an imitation of divine cosmic fecundity as well as our communication of our commitments to love and justice, to growth, and to communion with our partners, our community, our planet, the cosmos, and God. Our sexual interactions, as friends and embodiments of wholeness, strengthen and nourish both our own community and our communal compassion for all who are oppressed, for all who are suffering. Thus is our gay/lesbian identity and sensibility a prophetic mode of being-in-the-world.

Of course, to affirm the radical potential for wholeness in our gay/lesbian sexuality is also to pro- visionally assert that we can indeed live within para- dox, within creativity-begetting tension. A paradigm of friendship, for example, need not undermine sexual diversity, but it should help us to avoid a compulsive promiscuity. It can help us to discern some middle ground between reckless promiscuity and hetero-mono- gamy, and thereby enable us to join Silverstein (1981) in affirming all of our options:

> Gay men [and lesbians] need not apologize for [nonmonogamous] couple arrangement[s], nor should those who prefer exclusive [monogamous] arrange- ments be made to believe that they are in the mi- nority and somehow strange. Normative behavior should not be viewed as a rule or ideal. Diver- sity in the gay world has always been one of its strengths, and making rigid new rules to replace rigid old rules is not the way to improve our lives. (p. 339)

Affirming our diversity, therefore, means respecting and supporting the parameters of monogamous couples while constructing both our nonmonogamous partnerships and the variety of our uncoupled life in accord with the (com)passion and obligations of friendship.

A sexual ethics of friendship still allows us a variety of options. Monogamy remains a legitimate op- tion for us, for example, if it does not become either a withdrawal from sociopolitical involvement in gay/ lesbian community and activism or a reflection of our fears of our peers. While long term monogamy con- structed with utter equality and without gender roles can attest to the fact that intimacy and friendship can develop together--that long term deepened intimacy (friendship) need not undercut eroticism (sexual ful- fillment)--a defensive and/or paranoid monogamy only reinforces the myths of gay promiscuity and relational instability (cf., Berzon, 1988). Nonmonogamous part- ners must consequently meet additional and difficult tests, at once honoring and respecting other couples' limits (whether monogamous or nonmonogamous); nurturing the primary partners against the demons of jealousy, envy, and low self-esteem and toward optimal intimacy and genuine interdependence; and, befriending their outside partners while not undermining their primary

relationships. Uncoupled gay men and lesbians are, of
course, the most free to create various forms and networks of sexual interactions.

Regardless of all our options, however, the absolute value of friendship continues to resonate through
these theological and ethical reflections. The paradigm of friendship can be a workable model for constructing all of our sexual relationships, particularly
if we can increasingly insist that deepening intimacy
and eroticism need not be mutually exclusive. McNeill
(1988) has reminded us, for example, that "our struggle
. . . is above all else a struggle for the freedom to
love . . . a struggle to break free from all the obstacles to love and intimacy," as we simultaneously
(re)claim and (re)embrace the utter trustworthiness and
intrinsic value of our gayselves, our sexuality, and
our interrelationships (p. 205). Genuine fidelity in
our sexuality, in fact, grows from our sexual befriending to create and sustain the erotic nature and power
of our gay/lesbian community; our befriended relationships, for example, already inform and empower our sociopolitical activism and our AIDS-related care-giving.

The challenge to live within paradox and to create
wholeness therein also has profoundly personal implica-
tions, disclosing at once the provisional/confessional,
and thus idiosyncratic, side of this now public pilgrimage. To make such a confession remains an invitation
to dialogue, encouraging us to come together and to
help one another both to articulate and to construct
the "how" of our lives as gay men and lesbians. What I
want to attempt to do, then, is to stand firmly between
the opposites and even between the categories we ourselves have constructed, as gay men and lesbians enculturated by patriarchy. I want to affirm my desire to
wear leather, for example, as a symbol of my efforts to
heal my own "battered masculinity" (cf., Mains, 1984),
while simultaneously increasing my sensitivity to the
problems of male socialization and affirming feminist
or nonsexist goals. I want to affirm the radical potential of my sexuality and being-in-the-world and to
celebrate the strong bonds of friendship I see in the
leather community, particularly now in the face of
AIDS. I want to symbolize and to enact my wholistic
desire to be spiritually, psychically, physically,
(com)passionately, and yes, playfully engaged, flesh-
to-flesh, with another man. And, on those occasions
when I forego the tools and accessories of S/M in the
process, I do so simply because I do not want to break

the powerful and thoroughly tactile psycho-physical bond of our passionate sexual encounter.

I also want to resist labels and to exchange either/or for both/and in all my thinking-being-doing: I want to be able to be as tender and gentle as I am passionate, to be both sexual and reflective, embodied and spiritual. I want to break through the barriers which equate leather solely with pain, or misogyny, or a masculinity which excludes others. I want to affirm and celebrate my own idiosyncratic mix of gender attributes, of emotions and desires, of perceptions, reflections, and sexual expressions and, in seeking to create a provisional and ever-changing wholeness, to enact my empathy with all persons who struggle under patriarchy. And, yes, I would most prefer to hold all these things together--to embody and enact them--within the context of a monogamous covenant, not out of a genitally possessive fear of abandonment, but rather from a desire for an ever deepening psycho-spiritual-physical intimacy which focuses our power both inwardly for our spiritual growth and development together and outwardly for our empowered commitments to our community and to the world. Overall, then, I want to walk modestly and yet sure of foot on the tightrope, on the very margins of our marginality itself. In doing so, I believe I can embrace a paradigm of playful, committed, and loving friendship to inform my sexuality; I can open myself to the "power of freedom and newness of life," to God's "new possibilities" disclosed thereby (Ruether, 1985, p. 175); and, I can conjoin theory and praxis in the shared activism of my erotic community, as together we nurture one another and work to create justice, both in our relationships and in the world. I begin to believe--truly, deeply, fundamentally--that our gay/lesbian being-in-the-world and our sexual friendships are absolutely good and sacred. I come to realize that I am indeed a trustworthy celebrant . . . and I am both humbled and awed, and at last enabled to rejoice!

* * *

In the very face of AIDS and the persistent homophobia which AIDS in our community has only strengthened for our detractors, our defiant celebration is richly deserved and long overdue. And yet, paradoxically in and through its intrinsic value for us, our celebration is not just an end in itself, but a focusing of our pilgrimage and a point of further transition, a rite of passage. As our mythic and archetypal co-celebrants of gay/lesbian identity and sexuality retire and the glowing embers of our spent fires fade before the advance of dawn, we come into our full power and also into our full responsibility. Ultimately, the empowerment of our reclaimed wholeness, of our sexual celebration as an erotic community, and of our unified psychic/spiritual/physical renewal, returns (rebirths) us into the world, in order for us to resume an active, and even radical, participation in transforming and healing the world. We do not go forth into the world unprepared, however, for we return to the world ourselves transformed and healed, at once sustained by our numinous sexual friendships and buoyed on the arms of a divine cosmic embrace.

*   *   *

VIII. Apendices

(a) Safe-Sex Guidelines

The following listing represents a sample compilation of safe-sex guidelines as formulated by the major AIDS services and educational organizations in the U.S. Because some of these activities are subjects of controversy among both the medical and gay communities, and because AIDS research continues to proceed apace, readers should also consult their local AIDS support organization and keep abreast of changes regarding the status of specific activities.

Considered Safe

>   Dry kissing
>   Hugging, body rubbing, massage
>   Light S/M (without bleeding or bruising)
>   Mutual masturbation
>   Sex toys (when used only on oneself)
>   Sexual fantasies

Considered Possibly Safe (Low-Risk)

>   Anal or vaginal intercourse with a condom
>   Cunnilingus
>   Fisting with surgical gloves
>   French or deep kissing
>   Sucking/"69" (but stopping before orgasm)
>   Water sports (external only)

Considered Unsafe (High-Risk)

>   Anal or vaginal intercourse without a condom
>   Fisting without surgical gloves
>   Rimming
>   Sharing enema/douching equipment or sex toys
>   Sharing IV needles
>   Swallowing semen
>   Water sports (in mouth or on skin with sores
>   or cuts)

(b) Open Relationship Guidelines

The following guidelines and/or guideline-shaping questions are adapted from the survey findings of McWhirter and Mattison (1984, pp. 258-259). In **no** sense exhaustive, these preliminary guidelines and questions are included here simply as provisional suggestions to assist couples in the process of becoming more explicitly reflective and openly communicative about the choice of monogamy vs. nonmonogamy. As such, they can potentially further enable the responsible and purposive construction and long term maintenance of compassionate, ideally unthreatening, and nondehumanizing open relationships by gay/lesbian individuals who choose both to be a (primary) couple and also to be nonmonogamous. Obviously, no couple is likely to attempt to use all of these guidelines as phrased here; the individuals in any coupling must work together to establish flexible and renegotiable ground rules which will uniquely work for their specific relationship over time (cf., Berzon, 1988). In offering their version of these guidelines, McWhirter and Mattison (1984) preface them by indicating that while "developing a set of ground rules was reported to be very helpful" for the male couples in their survey, the guidelines in themselves do not adequately convey the "anguish, pain, hurt, and heartache" that often accompany the process and changes involved in deciding to construct a nonmonogamous relationship, particularly for gay/lesbian couples moving from previous monogamy into nonmonogamy, the motivations for which also require careful scrutiny (p. 258). Nevertheless, McWhirter and Mattison (1984) reiterate that reflectively, responsibly, and purposefully constructing nonmonogamy, through ongoing interpersonal dialogue between primary partners, consistently proves far more tenable than unwittingly shifting into (or, worse, inadvertently discovering) nonmonogamous behavior and then trying to reckon with the consequences. Some guidelines and questions, then, are as follows:

(1) **No** unsafe or high-risk sexual activities will be engaged in.

(2) Primary partners should attempt to reach a consensus _in advance_ as to whether outside sexual encounters will subsequently be shared and discussed with each other, and in what detail and when; setting a time-frame in advance for (re)-

evaluating a couple's open relationship ground rules may also prove helpful.

(3)   Outside sexual encounters should not interfere with the primary couple's customary routine or planned time together; they should especially not interfere with holidays or other special occasions; and, primary partners should return to each other at the most opportune/convenient time which both avoids dehumanizing an outside partner and best facilitates restoring the primary relationship's grounding and dynamics.

(4)   Outside sex is permissible only when primary partners are geographically separated for an extended period of time (over night? over a weekend? longer?).

(5)   Outside sex is permissible only with the prior agreement of one's primary partner, per each opportunity which arises.

(6)   While outside sexual encounters should be compassionate and humanizing, no emotional entanglements should be encouraged which might prove threatening to the primary relationship.

(7)   Secondary emotional relationships with sexual friends are permissible, but one's primary partner is never to be excluded or made to feel otherwise uncomfortable by such a friendship.

(8)   No sex with mutual friends is permissible (unless all three individuals can come together sexually without any inequities in attention and affection?).

(9)   Outside sexual encounters are not permissible in the home (?) or bedroom (?) of the primary partners (unless within a group situation which includes both primary partners equally?).

(10) Outside sexual activities and/or the search for outside partners should not become compulsive or consume inordinate amounts of a couple's socially recreational time; if they begin to do so, the primary couple should consider such behavior symptomatic and suspend outside sexual activities

to resolve either individual problems and/or problems within the primary relationship.

(11) When either primary partner experiences a prolonged threat as a result of the other's outside sexual activities or sexual friendships, outside sexual activities should be suspended until the primary partners resolve their personal and/or intrarelationship problems; importantly, suspending outside sexual activities may occasionally prove invaluable for (re)nurturing and sustaining the primary relationship.

(12) All sexual behavior both within and outside any primary relationship should be shaped by the paradigm of responsible and compassionate friendship (see chapters 3[iv] and 5, above), in an effort always to embody/enact genuine fidelity (see chapter 4[ii], above).

As indicated in chapter 3, above, constructing and sustaining long term nonmonogamy requires that primary partners always be willing to deal with tension, to work on feelings of jealousy and envy, and to sort out those issues from issues of self-esteem. It also means exploring and developing idiosyncratic ground rules which seek to create an ideal balance which transcends both genital possessiveness and any dehumanization of outside partners. Whether such a balancing act is truly possible, if we as gay men and lesbians are genuinely freed from the hetero-monogamous model, we then ultimately bear the responsibility for constructing our relationships, and our sexual behavior, in ways which enable us to be genuinely faithful friends and lovers. Therein lies the possibility of celebration.

* * *

IX. Notes

I. A Pilgrimage toward Celebration

[1]A noteworthy exception involves the recent work of the Lesbian/Feminist Issues in Religion Group of the American Academy of Religion. With a theme of "Relationship Ethics and Lesbian Experience," group members presented the following papers during the November 1988 AAR annual meetings in Chicago: "Celebrating Lesbianism: Transforming Ethical Foundations" (Mykel Johnson, Episcopal Divinity School); "The Pleasures, Integrity, and Freedom of the Body: Reclaiming the Body in the Age of AIDS" (Elizabeth A. Castelli, College of Wooster); and "Three Guilts/Three Sins (A Philosophico-Religious Duet)" (Cheshire Calhoun, College of Charleston, and Kathy Rudy, Duke University). The present text hopes to nurture similar dialogue within the gay male community.

II. Human Sexuality and Patriarchal Socialization

[2]For a detailed examination of St. Aelred's "theology of passionate friendship" and the mystical union of God with same-sex lovers, see Clark (1987), as well as chapter 5(ii), below.

[3]Evans (1988) risks simplistically blaming all the ills of the gay male subculture upon the gay ghetto and particularly upon the gay bar network. To do so fails to acknowledge that long ago patriarchy and homophobia drove gay men and lesbians, our lives and our special talents underground. As a result, our oppressed community shaped a subculture whose temples and town halls and social clubs became the gay bars and the realm of the night, where/when we could dare to gather for fellowship and mutual support, as well as for loving sexuality. Two brief decades of above-ground daylit gay liberation have not displaced this particular center of our communal being. While we are increasingly open and visible throughout society and in the struggles both for gay rights and for an adequate public response to AIDS at all levels, our subculture is still very much

shaped by and consigned to spaces and times which are nonthreatening to the heterosexual majority. Importantly, the gay subculture's response to AIDS, often with the active support of the bar network's owners as well as its patrons, has taught us that we can transform gay baths into health centers and gay bars into gathering places which are more socially and communally mutual and less sexually objectifying (cf., Clark, 1989). While our ghettoes and gay bars must not be above responsible/compassionate self-criticism, as discussed throughout the present text, we must also realize our need for gay spaces on the margins of heterosexual acceptability as the physical locations of our celebrations of gay life, of our fund-raising activities during the AIDS crisis, and of our continued politicization and empowerment for our liberation struggles, as from the Stonewall Inn in 1969. Furthermore, we must also increasingly assume responsibility for reshaping our subculture, including the gay bar network, in ways which will resist further shaping by heterosexism, as we move into an increasingly liberational future.

[4] For an extended discussion both of the ways in which genuine gay sexual wholeness and balance might function to undermine all other fundamental dualisms and to reconcile the cosmic and moral polarities (transcendence/immanence, spirit/matter, sacred/profane) and of one particular historical, non-Judaeo-Christian embodiment of such utter balance (the native American berdache), see Clark (1987, 1989), as well as Williams (1986) and Roscoe (1987).

III. Monogamy, Nonmonogamy, and Other Related Issues

[5] At this point of clear relationship crisis, where non-sexual problems and problems related to outside sexual activity have become confused and the primary relationship seems more full of tension and pain than love and hope, DeCecco and Shively (1988) urge couples back to negotiating, to communicating clearly and compassionately about needs, to sorting and reprioritizing, and to resolving the real problems and renewing the relationship. Failing that, Mendola (1980) counsels both a planned and compassionate separation, as the path to healing and growth for the newly uncoupled partners, and the development of a network of truly supportive (not merely co-grieving) friends. She insists that while the ability to live and to grow together may end, the love itself need not. The positive

love and other qualities of a good but terminated relationship can positively inform both oneself and one's
future relationships.

V. Sexual and Relational Models and Alternatives

[6] While same-sex friendships among men and their
theological/ethical value have been but infrequently
discussed, feminist theology has already examined and
(re)valued friendships among women; see, for example,
Raymond (1986).

VI. Radical Sexuality: Leathersex and S/M

[7] Because leathersex and S/M participants live as a
marginalized subgroup on the edges of an already marginalized subculture, disdained even by much of that
larger group, they often must undergo a "second coming
out," a further process of self-discovery and self-acceptance and of confrontation with yet other social
taboos, animal instincts, and human power and its
abuses. Self-identity with leathersex and/or S/M requires previous gayself-acceptance while it, at least
symbolically, takes gay distinctiveness a further defiant step away from hetero-assimilation (much like some
transvestism). As a result, leathersex, S/M, and their
participants become potent symbols of the socially outcast whom a gay/lesbian liberation theology and ethics
should champion (cf., Clark, 1985, Mains, 1984, 1987).

* * *

X. Literature Cited

Barbadette, G. (1982). The social triumph of the sexual will: A conversation with Michel Foucault. Trans. B. Lemon. Christopher Street, no. 64, 36-41.

Barrett, E. M. (1978). Gay people and moral theology. In L. Crew (Ed.), The gay academic (pp. 329-334). Palm Springs: Etc.

Bauman, B. (1983). Women-identified women in male-identified Judaism. In S. Heschel (Ed.), On being a Jewish feminist: A reader (pp. 88-95). New York: Schocken.

Berzon, B. (1988). Permanent partners: Building gay and lesbian relationships that last. New York: Dutton.

Boswell, J. (1980). Christianity, social tolerance, and homosexuality. Chicago: Univ. Chicago.

Boyd, M. (1984). Take off the masks. Philadelphia: New Society.

---. (1987). Telling a lie for Christ? In M. Thompson (Ed.), Gay spirit: Myth and meaning (pp. 78-87). New York: St. Martin's.

Christ, C. P. (1979). Spiritual quest and women's experience. In C. P. Christ & J. Plaskow (Eds.), Womanspirit rising: A feminist reader in religion (pp. 228-245). San Francisco: Harper & Row.

---. (1980). Diving deep and surfacing: Women writers on spiritual quest. Boston: Beacon.

Christ, C. P. & Plaskow, J. (1979). Introduction(s). In C. P. Christ & J. Plaskow (Eds.), Womanspirit rising: A feminist reader in religion (pp. 1-24, 63-67, 131-135, 193-197). San Francisco: Harper & Row.

Clark, J. M. (1985, December 2). The value of leathersex for an inclusive gay spirituality. The News (Atlanta Gay Center), 1(24), 11.

---. (1987). Gay being, divine presence: Essays in gay spirituality. Garland, TX: Tanglewüld.

---. (1989). A Place to start: Toward an unapologetic gay liberation theology. Dallas: Monument.

Collins, S. D. (1974). A different heaven and earth. Valley Forge: Judson.

---. (1979). Theology in the politics of Appalachian
women. In C. P. Christ & J. Plaskow (Eds.), Woman-
spirit rising: A feminist reader in religion (pp.
149-158). San Francisco: Harper & Row.
---. (1981). Feminist theology at the crossroads.
Christianity and Crisis, 41(20),342-347.
Daniel, W. (1950). Life of Aelred of Rievaulx. Trans.
F. M. Powicke. London: T. Nelson.
DeCecco, J. P. (1988). Obligation versus aspiration. In
J. P. DeCecco (Ed.), Gay relationships (pp. 1-10).
New York: Harrington Park.
DeCecco, J. P. & Shively, M. G. (1988). A study of per-
ceptions of rights and needs in interpersonal con-
flicts in homosexual relationships. In J. P. De-
Cecco (Ed.), Gay relationships (pp. 257-271). New
York: Harrington Park.
Doustourian, A. (1978). Gayness: A radical Christian
approach. In L. Crew (Ed.), The gay academic (pp.
335-349). Palm Springs: Etc.
Edwards, G. R. (1984). Gay/lesbian liberation: A bibli-
cal perspective. New York: Pilgrim.
Evans, A. (1988). The god of ecstasy: Sex-roles and the
madness of Dionysos. New York: St. Martin's.
Fackenheim, E. L. (1968). Quest for past and future:
Essays in Jewish theology. Bloomington: Indiana
Univ.
Fortunato, J. E. (1983). Embracing the exile: Healing
journeys of gay Christians. New York: Seabury.
---. (1987). AIDS, the spiritual dilemma. San Francisco: Harper & Row.
Fox, M. (1983). The spiritual journey of the homosexual
. . . and just about everyone else. In R. Nugent
(Ed.), A challenge to love: Gay and lesbian Catho-
lics in the church (pp. 189-204). New York: Cross-
road.
Gallagher, B. & Wilson, A. (1987). Sex and the politics
of identity: An interview with Michel Foucault. In
M. Thompson (Ed.), Gay spirit: Myth and meaning
(pp. 25-35). New York: St. Martin's.
Goodman, G., et al. (1983). No turning back: Lesbian &
gay liberation for the '80s. Philadelphia: New Society.
Hallier, A. (1969). The monastic theology of Aelred of
Rievaulx. Trans. C. Heaney. Shannon: Irish Univ.
Harry, J. (1988). Decision making and age differences
among gay male couples. In J. P. DeCecco (Ed.),
Gay relationships (pp. 117-132). New York: Har-
rington Park.

Hay, H. (1987). A separate people whose time has come. In M. Thompson (Ed.), Gay spirit: Myth and meaning (pp. 279-291). New York: St. Martin's.

Heyward, I. C. (1982). The redemption of God: A theology of mutual relation. Washington: Univ. Pr. America.

---. (1984). Our passion for justice: Images of power, sexuality, and liberation. New York: Pilgrim.

Horner, T. (1978). Jonathan loved David: Homosexuality in biblical times. Philadelphia: Westminster.

Jones, R. W. & Bates, J. E. (1988). Satisfaction in male homosexual couples. In J. P. DeCecco (Ed.), Gay relationships (pp. 237-245). New York: Harrington Park.

Kurdek, L. A. & Schmitt, J. P. (1988). Relationship quality of gay men in closed or open relationships. In J. P. DeCecco (Ed.), Gay relationships (pp. 217-234). New York: Harrington Park.

Laner, M. R. (1988). Permanent partner priorities: Gay and straight. In J. P. DeCecco (Ed.), Gay relationships (pp. 133-155). New York: Harrington Park.

Lee, J. A. (1988). Forbidden colors of love: Patterns of gay love and gay liberation. In J. P. DeCecco (Ed.), Gay relationships (pp. 11-32). New York: Harrington Park.

Mains, G. (1984). Urban aboriginals: A celebration of leathersexuality. San Francisco: Gay Sunshine.

---. (1987). Urban aboriginals and the celebration of leather magic. In M. Thompson (Ed.), Gay spirit: Myth and meaning (pp. 99-117). New York: St. Martin's.

Marcus, E. (1988). The male couple's guide to living together. New York: Harper and Row.

McNeill, J. J. (1983). Homosexuality, lesbianism, and the future: The creative role of the gay community in building a more humane society. In R. Nugent (Ed.), A challenge to love: Gay and lesbian Catholics in the church (pp. 52-64). New York: Crossroad.

---. (1987, March 11). Homosexuality: Challenging the church to grow. The Christian Century, pp. 242-246.

---. (1988). Taking a chance on God: Liberating theology for gays, lesbians, their lovers, families, and friends. Boston: Beacon.

McWhirter, D. P. & Mattison, A. M. (1984). The male couple: How relationships develop. Englewood Cliffs, NJ: Prentice-Hall.

---. (1988). Stages in the development of gay relation-
   ships. In J. P. DeCecco (Ed.), Gay relationships
   (pp. 161-167). New York: Harrington Park.
Mendola, M. (1980). The Mendola report: A new look at
   gay couples. New York: Crown.
Morton, N. (1985). The journey is home. Boston: Beacon.
Nelson, J. B. (1977). Homosexuality and the church.
   Christianity and Crisis, 37(5),63-69.
---. (1978). Embodiment: An approach to sexuality and
   Christian theology. Minneapolis: Augsburg.
Neusner, J. (1979). The tasks of theology in Judaism: A
   humanistic program. Journal of Religion, 59(1),71-
   86.
Peplau, L. A. (1988). Research on homosexual couples:
   An overview. In J. P. DeCecco (Ed.), Gay relation-
   ships (pp. 33-40). New York: Harrington Park.
Peplau, L. A. & Cochran, S. D. (1988). Value orientation in the intimate relationships of gay men. In
   J. P. DeCecco (Ed.), Gay relationships (pp. 195-
   216). New York: Harrington Park.
Plaskow, J. (1983). The right question is theological.
   In S. Heschel (Ed.), On being a Jewish feminist: A
   reader (pp. 223-233). New York: Schocken.
---. (1988, November 20). Toward a feminist theology of
   sexuality. Women & Religion Section, Amer. Academy
   of Religion, Chicago.
Raymond, J. G. (1986). A passion for friends: Toward a
   philosophy of female affection. Boston: Beacon.
Reece, R. & Segrist, A. E. (1988). The association of
   selected   "masculine"   sex-role   variables   with
   length of relationship in gay male couples. In J.
   P. DeCecco (Ed.), Gay relationships (pp. 177-194).
   New York: Harrington Park.
Roby, D. (Ed.). (1974). [Aelred of Rievaulx]. On spiri-
   tual friendship. Trans. M. E. Laker. Washington:
   Cistercian.
Roscoe, W. (1987). Living the tradition: Gay American
   Indians. In M. Thompson (Ed.), Gay spirit: Myth
   and meaning (pp. 69-77). New York: St. Martin's.
Rubenstein, R. L. (1966). After Auschwitz: Radical the-
   ology   and   contemporary   Judaism.   Indianapolis:
   Bobbs-Merrill.
Ruether, R. R. (1972). Liberation theology. New York:
   Paulist.
---. (1978). The sexuality of Jesus: What the synoptics
   have to say. Christianity and Crisis, 38(8),134-
   137.
---. (1983a). Sexism and God-talk: Toward a feminist
   theology. Boston: Beacon.

---. (1983b). To change the world: Christology and cultural criticism. New York: Crossroad.

---. (1985). Womanguides: Readings toward a feminist theology. Boston: Beacon.

Russell, K. C. (1982). Aelred, the gay abbot of Rievaulx. Studia Mystica, 5(4),51-64.

Satloff, C. R. (1983). History, fiction, and the tradition: Creating a Jewish feminist poetic. In S. Heschel (Ed.), On being a Jewish feminist: A reader (pp. 186-206). New York: Schocken.

Silverstein, C. (1981). Man to man: Gay couples in America. New York: Morrow/Quill.

Squire, A. (1981). Aelred of Rievaulx: A study. Kalamazoo, MI: Cistercian Publns.

Townsend, L. (1983). The leatherman's handbook II. New York: Modernismo.

Treblicot, J. (1984). Taking responsibility for sexuality. In R. Baker & F. Elliston (Eds.), Philosophy and sex (pp. 421-430). Buffalo: Prometheus.

Uhrig, L. J. (1984). The two of us: Affirming, celebrating, and symbolizing gay and lesbian relationships. Boston: Alyson.

Umansky, E. M. (1984). Creating a Jewish feminist theology: Possibilities and problems. Anima, 10(2), 125-135.

Walker, M. (1980). Visionary love: A spiritbook of gay mythology and transmutational faerie. San Francisco: Treeroots.

Williams, W. L. (1986). The spirit and the flesh: Sexual diversity in American Indian culture. Boston: Beacon.

* * *

XI. Index

*   *   *

Photo Credit: Kim Brokaw

Biographical Sketch

J. Michael Clark (B.A., Religion and Philosophy, Emory & Henry College, 1975; M.Div., Theological Studies, Candler School of Theology, Emory University, 1978; Ph.D., Literature-&-Theology and Gender Studies, Graduate Institute of the Liberal Arts, Emory University, 1983) is an "independent scholar" who has written numerous articles and books in gay studies, including work in socio-literary criticism, in constructive theology, and on pastoral care for persons-with-AIDS. Among his most pertinent work are Gay Being, Divine Presence: Essays in Gay Spirituality (Garland, TX: Tangelwüld Press, 1987) and A Place to Start: Toward an Unapologetic Gay Liberation Theology (Dallas: Monument Press, 1989).

* * *

DATE DUE